185 - experience as proof

198 - astus

208 = feelings & connection
to others.

210-11 Post - materialist

219-23 active imagination.
3 short techniques.

Advance Praise for This Book

Far From This Land:
A Memoir About Evolution, Love, and the Afterlife

"Michael Gellert's wonderful new book is a fine testament to the power of illness to transform us. An illness itself is an altered state of consciousness. I greatly admire Michael's ability to use his own struggles to help and to heal others. This book is a delightful treat for all of us who are fascinated by the incredible healing powers of the unconscious mind."
—RAYMOND A. MOODY, JR., M.D., PH.D., author of
Life After Life and research pioneer who
coined the term "near-death experience"

"A most unconventionally convincing story, so breathtaking that I had to periodically pause to come up for air."
—BARBARA BROWN TAYLOR, *New York Times* bestselling
author of *Holy Envy* and *Learning to Walk in the Dark*

"*Far From This Land* is a thoroughly enjoyable reading experience, rich with challenging insights and presented in a unique, down-to-earth, approachable manner. It's not exactly about philosophy or psychology or marriage, yet it wraps all these together into a single, enthralling story that gives the genre of magical realism a whole new meaning. It shows how the world is its own magic. I recommend this book most highly."
— GARY GRANGER, Humanities Professor Emeritus,
Vanier College, Montreal

"This is a remarkable book that sets in motion the dream-scape of the unconscious mind. Gellert applies Jung's active-imagination techniques with great originality. The evolutionary material is fascinating, taking a deep dive into the philosophy of theologian Pierre Teilhard de Chardin, among other things."

— WENDY GOLDMAN ROHM,
New York Times bestselling author

"*Far From This Land* is spellbinding and numinous. I live in Los Angeles where it almost never rains and even more rarely is there thunder and lightning. While I was reading this book, a thunderstorm appeared and a bolt of lightning struck a tree next to my home, causing the tree to fall only inches away from it. This was an apt metaphor for my experience reading this memoir. It is earth-shattering and extremely powerful, yet often light and funny. Filled with vivid, mesmerizing dreams and imagery, it is an important work that you will want to read and reread!"

— ANN WALKER, PH.D., Book Review Editor,
Psychological Perspectives: A Journal of Global Consciousness Integrating Psyche, Soul, and Nature

"Teilhard de Chardin once observed, 'matter is spirit slowed enough to be seen.' Michael Gellert's *Far From This Land* is an extraordinary exploration of the interweaving mysteries of the cosmos and of the human brain. Utilizing 'active imagination,' he challenges the historic splitting of spirit and matter and experiences a merging of the two in his dialogue with the disparate parts of the psyche. His story is a compelling *mystery* investigation, in the best sense of that word."

— JAMES HOLLIS, PH.D., Jungian analyst and author, most recently of *Living Between Worlds: Finding Personal Resilience in Changing Times*

"*Far From This Land* is one of the most profound and eloquent rebuttals of materialism to appear in this century. Psychoanalyst Michael Gellert's experience during brain surgery opened doors to the nature of consciousness foreshadowed in the works of Pierre Teilhard de Chardin and C. G. Jung. This book is a beautiful, towering accomplishment, and a powerful response to the challenges our species faces at this critical hinge of history."

— LARRY DOSSEY, M.D., author of *One Mind: How Our Individual Mind Is Part of a Greater Consciousness and Why It Matters*

"As a Jungian analyst, Gellert knew he had experienced something unique and he does not disappoint in the retelling of his extraordinary encounters. These accounts of his active imaginations in which he interrogates the conditions of an 'other-world' or other dimension are thoughtful and thought-provoking. It is brave work to bring such personal and intimate experiences to print and he does so with honesty of purpose and as a result we are able to journey with him. In many respects, Gellert's experience compares with Jung's own in equal exploration of the nature of dreams, visions and the meaning we make from them."

—STEPHANI L. STEPHENS, University of Canberra, Australia, author of *C. G. Jung and the Dead: Visions, Active Imagination and the Unconscious Terrain*

"I truly enjoyed Michael Gellert's impressive, compelling, and visionary story. He demonstrates the power of active imagination. Like Jung's *Red Book*, this book makes us think about reality in a new way, offering a window into realms of the psyche of which we are usually unaware. *Far From This Land* is also an inspiring act of courage and love in the face of serious illness."

—LIONEL CORBETT, M.D., professor of psychology, Pacifica Graduate Institute, and author of *The Religious Function of the Psyche*

"A miraculous book about a world just out of reach—or at least just out of reach when we are awake and sober—yet the source of inspiration for mystics and poets throughout history. It may upset your views on what is possible. Read it at your own risk!"

—ALLAN COMBS, PH.D., neuropsychologist, Director of the Center for Consciousness Studies at California Institute of Integral Studies, and author of *The Radiance of Being*

"The time has come for the return of the archetypes to our society. Author Michael Gellert has presented Jung's ideas on the archetypes in an original and evocative manner that, by itself, will captivate you. Additionally, you will learn something very important in the way that consciousness builds the world through us. Your waking up to the archetypes is the purpose for the play of consciousness."

—AMIT GOSWAMI, PH.D., quantum physicist, Professor Emeritus, University of Oregon, and author (with Valentina Onisor) of *Quantum Spirituality* and *The Quantum Brain*

"Why isn't humanity pulling together to navigate these apocalyptic times to create a better future? Racism, war, and obscene gaps in wealth divide us. A less obvious, even more fundamental evolutionary barrier to knowing our common human nature is the sharp conflict between science and religion, matter and spirit. This book is a call to imaginative self-discovery which anyone can find within their own psyche. Michael Gellert models the method for this in his captivating story of personal evolution through confrontation with our own inner divides. Great preparation for coming together at last!"

—ELISABET SAHTOURIS, PH.D., evolution biologist and futurist, *author of EarthDance: Living Systems in Evolution* and other titles on *sahtouris.com*

"In *Far From This Land*, Michael Gellert, a well-respected Jungian analyst, shares with us his near-death self-exploration through his work with his dreams, and he does so in a tender, instructive, and captivating way."

—PETER A. LEVINE, PH.D., author of *Waking the Tiger: Healing Trauma* and *In an Unspoken Voice: How the Body Releases Trauma and Restores Goodness*

Far From
This Land

Far From This Land

A Memoir About Evolution, Love, and the Afterlife

MICHAEL GELLERT

Nicolas Hays
Lake Worth, FL

Published in 2021 by Nicolas Hays, Inc.
P. O. Box 540206
Lake Worth, FL 33454-0206
www.nicolashays.com

Distributed to the trade by
Red Wheel/Weiser, LLC
65 Parker St. • Ste. 7
Newburyport, MA 01950
www.redwheelweiser.com

ISBN: 978-0-89254-196-6
Ebook ISBN: 978-0-89254-689-3

Library of Congress Cataloging-in-Publication Data
available upon request

Book design and production by Studio 31
www.studio31.com

Printed in the U.S.A. (MV)

For George, a brother in every sense of the meaning,
and for Noelle, the sister I never had

Perhaps there do indeed exist universes interpenetrating with ours; perhaps of a high complexity; perhaps containing their own forms of awareness; constructed out of other particles and other interactions than those we know now, but awaiting discovery through some common but elusive interaction that we have yet to spot. It is not the physicist's job to make this sort of speculation, but today, when we are so much less sure of the natural world than we were two decades ago, he can at least license it.

— Sir Denys Wilkinson, nuclear physicist

Sometimes, Number One, you just have to bow to the absurd.

— Jean-Luc Picard, captain of the USS Enterprise

OH WOW. OH WOW. OH WOW.

— Steve Jobs's final words on his deathbed

Contents

Author's Opening Remarks
How to Read This Book

The following story is based on a series of dreams I had in response to brain surgery and to facing my human frailty and mortality. It is the creative expression of what can happen when we consciously dream our dreams onward from where they ended. This can also involve protracted conversations with and among the inner figures who populate our dreams, conversations that produce penetrating insights into the dreams themselves and the vexing problems they are often about. Jung called this method of exploring the unknown "active imagination." It led not only to the creation of his *Red Book*—a remarkable account of his conversations with his own inner figures—but to what subsequently became of that project, namely, the foundation of all his later psychological works. Since this method is so central to our book, some preliminary discussion of it is warranted.

As Jung himself acknowledged, he did not invent this method. In the fourth century, Saint Augustine admitted in the opening lines of his philosophical inquiry, *Soliloquies*, that he was mystified by the way it developed as a dialogue with "Reason," the latter taking form as an inner voice that was not associated with a dream figure per se but that nevertheless suddenly spoke to him. Goethe is known to have written some of his poems in a somnambulistic, dream state, as if he were possessed, and he purposely secluded himself so as to foster this condition.

As did the Swedish filmmaker Ingmar Bergman, whose screenplay for his film *Hour of the Wolf* was inspired by inner figures who not only talked to him but, appearing externally as projections, wouldn't leave his room until the film was completed. (As contemporaries, Bergman was familiar with Jung but apparently not with his use of active imagination.) Similarly, Rainer Maria Rilke's mystical, prayer-like poems in his *Book of Hours* began with what he described as forceful "inner dictations" occurring in the mornings and evenings, the times when we are closest to sleep and the unconscious. (Rilke and Jung were familiar with each other, though Rilke was on more intimate terms with Freud.) But even a thinker as worldly as Thomas Jefferson clearly engaged in a self-reflective active imagination when he wrote his famous lyrical "dialogue between my Head and my Heart" as part of a letter to a married woman he fell in love with.

T. S. Eliot described the more shamanic side of active imagination as a "disciplined kind of dreaming" that has been forgotten in modern times but in earlier times was revered as the practice of seeing visions. (Visions would thus be dreams we cultivate while we are awake but in a meditative or trance state.) Coleridge understood this visionary discipline to be a way to participate in a "sacramental universe" or "imaginal realm transcending any personal existence," and he distinguished it from the creativity of the artist. *Active imagination is not fiction or novel writing*, even if at times it may resemble it because it gravitates toward expressive arts like sculpting, painting, poetry, playwriting, and creative nonfiction. Through them, it connects us to the deeper layers of the psyche, layers that, if their numinous effects on us are any indication, seem to border on otherworldly realms. Or perhaps, as William Blake and others intuited, *they are those realms themselves*—a possibility that this book entertains. This story is a memoir of my visits—via dreams and active imagination—to what appeared to be such realms.

As you may have guessed by now, this is an unorthodox memoir. To begin with, unlike most memoirs, it is shaped by psychological and spiritual events more than familial, social, or historical ones; that is to say, it's more inner-oriented and intrapersonal than outer-oriented and interpersonal. Then there is the distinct kind of psychological and spiritual memoir that it is. The figures in our dreams, as any of us can observe, have a will and agenda of their own. There's no predicting what they will say and do. The same is true for the active imagination we engage in with them. There's no telling in advance in which direction it may turn, and why. Dreaming and active imagination are both a suprarational process. The inner figures who drive both activities can assume an identity far different than our own, representing what Jung called "part-souls" or "splinter psyches"—subpersonalities or parts of our psychic constitution but not all of it. Their existence is natural and normal—we all have these parts—and they become a problem only when the ego or central personality becomes fragmented and overtaken by them in such extreme and rare conditions as dissociative or multiple personality disorder. The diverse religious traditions that have historically incorporated active imagination into their practices have always viewed it as a safe and productive way to investigate the mysteries of the human psyche and to tap into

Coleridge's sacramental or sacred universe. (Among such traditions, Jung includes the Jesuits with their Ignatian spiritual exercises, Patanjali's yoga with its sutras or aphorisms on the theory and practice of yoga, certain forms of Buddhist meditation, and medieval alchemy.) All the same, active imagination is not widely used as a way to tell one's personal story.

A further distinction making this memoir unusual is its main figure and narrator, a subpersonality—one so strong that it is practically an alter ego—named Richard Caldwell. His temperament, orientation, and biographical history are hardly my own. He personifies a skeptical side of me and gives voice to the existential doubts plaguing the period connected with my surgery, especially doubts about the continuity of consciousness after we die. In other words, the story is told from the critical, discerning perspective of a shrewd skeptic who is not easily fooled. That its narrator should be him rather than me was not a decision I consciously made. He spontaneously emerged in the post-surgical phase and insisted on telling the story—including all the dreams and visionary, active-imagination material that arose during this phase—from his point of view, essentially making it *his* story. What could I do, other than give him free rein? If repressed or cast out, he'd only return with greater forcefulness in his doubt.

Another figure, much closer to my conscious identity (or the actual ego), represents the professional part of me, the part informed by my profession as a Jungian psychoanalyst. The story very much unfolds as a dialogue between these two figures, my inner skeptic and my professional self. The first encounters a parallel universe (a.k.a. the afterlife), and the second, in the capacity of his analyst, helps him to make sense of this. The professional self becomes a helper or healer to the skeptical self, who in turn submits to the ordeal of psychotherapy. "Healer, heal thyself," as the ancient proverb says.

However, this analyst does not practice his craft entirely in the style I do. He often seems more like a didactic teacher than an analyst simply listening and gently fording the patient's inner process with him, trusting the psyche to find its own cure. He's quick to make interpretations and to explain to the patient the meaning of the latter's experiences, as if he knows better (and as it often happens, he does). In large measure, this is a creative device employed for narrative purposes, one whose use Jung would probably frown upon. He would agree that a psychopomp or spiritual guide is needed in order to clarify what the unconscious has revealed (often the guide is an agent or spokesperson for the unconscious, and in this story there is more than one), but he would disagree that this function should be the ego's. Citing Nietzsche's *Thus Spake Zarathustra* as an example of active imagination that is "too strongly consciously formed," Jung stresses the importance of carefully separating material in one's conscious mind from that of the unconscious. He believed that material seeping in from the ego or conscious mind waters down the objectivity of the unconscious and the active imagination that flows from it. The approach I take here is more in sync with the poets, playwrights, and philosophers who do not so finely distinguish between conscious and unconscious material and intentions. Either way, the conversations our inner figures have with each other or directly with us speak to the psyche's impulse to reveal itself and to work out its inner conflicts and self-dividedness. A tremendously transformative and integrative power is unleashed when we allow our inner parts to talk with each other.

Speaking of poets, as a record of visits to other realms, the book has some features in common with Dante's *Divine Comedy*—a fact I was unaware of during the process of writing it. Of course, I am not elevating my account to the level of Dante's eloquent, sublime, epic poem, mesmerizing us with its boundless, vivid imagery and layers of rich allegory. Merely, I am pointing to these basic features—six of them, to be exact—to illustrate how creativity of this kind can follow certain "grooves," suggesting the influence of what Jung understood as the archetypes of the collective unconscious. No writer is an island unto themselves.

(1) The first way my story resembles *The Divine Comedy* is that the latter is also, as Eliot and others contend, a product of active imagination. Both have the quality of a revelation, a novel disclosure yet also a perennial truth. Like many exercises in active imagination, both stories wrestle with religious, philosophical, spiritual, and psychological themes.

(2) Second, Dante and I are both actors in our stories—such participation being a general feature of active imagination—and we are both portrayed as alternate versions of ourselves. In Dante's case, he is presented as an idealized version he would have liked to have been. In my case, I'm presented in two versions that, as dis-

cussed above, reflect exaggerated parts of me, one that is a skeptic in matters of ultimate truth, and the other a loquacious, proactive psychoanalyst. I'm afraid neither of these alternate versions is as attractive as Dante's.

Third, if we compare Dante's journey through Hell, Purgatory, and Paradise (or Heaven) to most modern near-death experiences (admittedly, perhaps an unfair comparison), we see a sharp difference in purpose. Dante's allegorical visit to the other side of the grave is primarily *instructive*, aiming to illuminate how to live a moral and spiritual life that leads to God or Heaven rather than to Purgatory or Hell. In contrast to the modern near-death experience, it was not intended to provide emotional comfort and facilitate safe passage back to the land of the living. It was not a short, single-episode event but a learning process unfolding over the course of a week, precisely, the week beginning on the night before Good Friday in the year 1300. Though the story told in this book is about a modern near-death experience, it likewise aspires to be educative and process-oriented, but naturally with a different perspective and different themes than characteristic of Dante's medieval Catholic theology. *(Gellert's)*

Fourth, the fact that this story begins darkly yet concludes with a kind of redemption and a hopeful outlook further gives it something in common with Dante's journey. This qualifies both stories as comedy—"comedy" as understood in the ancient, classical sense of the meaning—as opposed to tragedy whose movement is from light to darkness.

(5) Fifth, given this comedic feature, it is noteworthy that the redemption in both stories is spearheaded by male guides (in Dante's instance, the Roman poet Virgil) but is finally midwifed or consummated by extraordinary women who are the love interests of the narrators. As we shall see, a man's female, inner figures tend to serve as a bridge to the hidden depths of the psyche, or to what the ancients called the soul. With its diverse characteristics, this feminine side within every man is what Jung referred to as the anima.

(6) Lastly, another core feature that the two stories share is their concern for ordinary life in the everyday world we inhabit. It should be remembered that Dante did not intend his *Commedia* to be only an exaltation or mystical contemplation of otherworldly realms. (Indeed, the adjective *Divina* was added after he died.) He also intended it to be a reflection upon the condition of the mundane world that he lived in, namely, the Christian world around the year 1300. So, too, does this story explore questions about an afterlife as a means to raise our awareness about how we should choose to live here and now in *our* world and century. It is, at heart, a story about *this* world, this Earth we dwell upon—in Dante's words, "The small round floor that makes us passionate . . ."

On a final note, it is worth repeating that the book is a memoir. It is a faithful rendition of what the psyche released when its intimate partner, the brain, was intruded upon and when my natural fragility as a mere mortal was stripped down to a stark naked vulnerability. The dreams and visionary, active-imagination experiences in the story are described in the way they happened. They are events as real or true as any, only they represent the reality or truth of the psyche. Specifically, they represent the part of the psyche that appears to be able to perceive higher or otherworldly realms, or, again, to perhaps be those realms itself. This memoir is about my visits to this distant region of the psyche, where the mind evidently meets and merges with these realms.

—Michael Gellert
Los Angeles, 2021

Prelude
Initial Consultation and
Considerations

April, 2007

The story I wish to tell must begin with the confession that I am the least likely person to tell it. Until recently, I had always been an atheist who had no difficulty believing in religious experiences. I just didn't believe they were outside the scope of natural phenomena. As a professor of evolutionary psychology, I often repeated to my students the fact that nothing in physical nature shows any evidence that it is designed by something beyond itself. Even so, nature is extremely complex and beautiful, and my awe of it was similar to the kind expressed by Einstein and Spinoza. If that love of nature is what people mean by the love of God, then you could say I had this too. But the notion of a superior intelligence transcending nature was never one I could wrap my mind around. Today, my confidence that this notion is purely wishful thinking has been shaken. And confidence it was: as someone once said, it takes great faith to be an atheist. I have become a man who has lost his faith.

If you think this is a simple problem you are mistaken. Losing one's faith in the idea that the ultimate meaning of existence is what humans give it is no small matter. This conviction cannot be easily and welcomingly replaced by some newfound religious belief. It may be far easier to lose belief in a God or a heaven than, after a lifetime of scientific training and atheism, to gain one. How does one develop a religious understanding that is as sophisticated and sober, as intricate and clear, as the laws of nature which one previously held as the highest order? Believers who have lost their faith may seek help from a priest or some wise person who perhaps once also suffered such a crisis, but to whom do nonbelievers turn when they lose their faith?

I had been told of a Jungian psychoanalyst who had formerly been a therapist at my university. A colleague had consulted him to get help for her anxiety. In addition to his specialty of working with dreams as a way to understand the unconscious mind and our patterns of behavior, she had told me he was interested in mysticism and had studied with a Zen master in Japan. I had the impression that he was "out there" on the fringes of psychology. It thus seemed likely that he would not be one to think I was crazy. If consulting him did not yield any insight as to what caused my experience, then perhaps I'd get some clues as to what did not.

I left a message for him on his voicemail. He called back shortly and gave me an appointment. Due to my operation I was still on a light schedule with no classes to teach. Though officially still on medical leave, I was feeling well enough to meet with him. Besides, I needed something to do. Staying at home and catching up on my reading didn't work. I couldn't concentrate. Likewise, the paper I had begun to write before the operation no longer held my interest. My mind kept returning to what happened during my surgery.

We met and shook hands. His name was Michael Gellert, and I could see he was a friendly man. He was in his early or mid-fifties, a good twelve to fifteen years older than me.

We sat down, I on a couch and he in a chair opposite me. Two bookcases were lined with books on a variety of subjects, though mostly psychology and religion. After some small talk and discussion about my livelihood—I mentioned that I was fortunate to be a professor of evolutionary psychology in one of the few university psychology departments to host a chair specifically in this subject—I told him about my surgery. He asked how I discovered something was wrong with me.

"About four days before the operation," I said, "I developed a terrible headache and felt very fatigued. And nauseous. At first I thought I was just overtired. By the third day it got so bad I had to go to the emergency room. I thought my head was going to split open. They took blood tests, a CAT scan, and kept me overnight. The next thing I know the neurosurgeon is in my room, discussing options. There weren't any. It was an aneurysm, and I went under the knife the next day."

An aneurysm is caused by a weakness in the wall of an artery, causing the vessel to widen and potentially hemorrhage. If this should happen inside the skull, it can cause permanent damage. Mine had only leaked. To repair the vessel, they opened the cranium around my right ear and went inside.

"How did the surgery go?"

"Before the surgery, it was bleeding only a little. It hadn't fully ruptured. A little over halfway through, it burst. In trying to control the bleeding by clamping the vessel, my brain was deprived of oxygen for over four minutes. They put me in a pentobarbital coma to lower my brain's oxygen requirement. The doctor told me later that I was at risk of catastrophic brain damage. I was in surgery for fourteen hours."

Gellert asked if there were any complications after the surgery. I told him that for about six weeks following the surgery, I was at risk of stroke from vasospasm from the bleeding that occurred around my brain. I fortunately didn't have one and there were no lasting complications. In five years I would need an angiogram just to make sure that everything is okay.

"It must have been a frightening experience," Gellert said.

"Frankly, it all happened so fast I hardly had time to get scared."

I didn't know if this was the right moment to go into the real disturbance for which I came to get his help.

After a brief pause he asked if I was married. I told him my wife and I had separated about a month before all this happened, and that it was a trial separation.

"I had already moved out and was in my own place," I said. "Naturally, she was shocked and upset when she learned I needed brain surgery. But she came through for me. Karen was there throughout the whole ordeal. She wanted me to recuperate in our house, but for one reason or another I preferred to go to my apartment. My brother flew in from D.C. just before I was discharged and together they helped out the first few weeks."

He asked if I had any kids. Two, I told him. "Rachel is six, Ben is four."

Then he asked, "How are they doing with all this? Surgery, separation, that's a lot."

"It's been hard on them. Endless questions. We answer them as best as we can. We shielded them as much as possible from the surgery. But when they saw me four days after with my head all bandaged, they got very upset."

"Understandably. Tell me, what has your mood been like these days?"

"I've been in a malaise. I feel listless most of the time, and when I'm not listless, I'm agitated."

"Is that unusual for you?"

"Yes, I would say so."

"And you've been like that since the operation?"

"Yes."

"Would you say you're depressed?"

"I don't know."

"What are you feeling right now?"

"I don't know, nothing really."

A silence descended upon us.

"How do you think I can help you, Richard?" he finally said.

"I'll tell you. I had a strange experience when I was under the anesthesia, and I need someone to talk to about it. I think you might be the guy who can help me with this."

He stared at me. It seemed as if he was surprised.

31

"What kind of experience?" he said.

"I don't exactly know. That's why I'm coming to you."

"Was it an NDE—a near-death experience?"

"You're asking if I saw a tunnel with light at the end, and a guide and loved ones waiting there to greet me?"

"Yes."

"No. It wasn't that. It was much stranger. It lasted for what seemed like hours. It could be my sense of time was warped, but that is how it felt."

"During the operation, did you flatline?"

"No. It wasn't a typical near-death experience. I looked through the literature. It wasn't anything like that."

"Have you told anyone about this—your surgeon?"

"I mentioned it to him. He thought it was a hypnagogic occurrence connected with the pentobarbital. I didn't go into it any further as I didn't think he'd understand. So no, I didn't tell anyone, not even my wife. You're the first."

Now we both quietly stared at each other.

I thought about his question, *how could he help me?* I had never been to a therapist or felt that someone could help me in personal matters better than I could help myself. The fact that I didn't really know how he could help me merely reflected that I couldn't help myself. I had no idea of what help would look like in such an instance.

It was only my second week driving again since the operation. I drove home late that afternoon wondering if confiding in Gellert was the right thing to do. I knew he would treat our discussion with the utmost confidence and respect, but I was concerned about making an already incomprehensible matter even more incomprehensible. His line of questioning in connection to near-death experiences concerned me. Yes, I had been in a perilous situation, and in that regard you might say I had a close brush with death. But I did not want him to squeeze my experience into the category of an NDE if there were other ways to also understand it.

On the other hand, I had the impression that Gellert would be an empathic and open-minded listener. At the end of our consultation, we agreed to an open series of meetings that would explore the experience I had. Given its lengthy duration, he asked that I write it down from beginning to end, even if it took a number of weeks and installments. He also wanted me to report any dreams I had during the course of our sessions.

I was relieved to have someone knowledgeable with whom I could talk. I was hoping our sessions might give some structure to the state of malaise I had fallen into.

When I arrived back at my apartment, Rachel and Ben were waiting for me. Karen was there too. Twice a week she dropped them off to stay with me. Since the operation, this too was only the second week that I was well enough to have them stay overnight.

"Did you see the therapist?" Karen asked after I greeted her and the kids. She knew I was going to meet him, but didn't know the real reason why. I had told her I was going to see him to talk about my malaise.

"Yes."

"What did he say?"

"He wants to see me again. We're going to meet every Tuesday."

"Good," she said, as she walked to the door. She kissed me on the cheek and told me to call her if I had any difficulties.

My understanding of the rift that led to our separation was murky. After nine years of marriage, it was no longer the day-to-day differences that taxed our relationship. That Karen is a morning person and I'm not, that she's rather sociable and I'm not, that she's highly structured with family events and plans and I'm not—we've learned to accommodate those differences and compromise as much as possible. Our drifting apart has rather been in our values and priorities. Some years ago Karen had a religious awakening to which, frankly, I could not relate. As time went on, we had less and less to talk about. Our taste in books, movies, and weekend activities increasingly diverged. We liked to hike and ski together, but I had little interest in yoga and Buddhist meditation. She often expressed how she found my approach to life joyless and pessimistic, particularly my belief that the human race is very likely heading toward an evolutionary crisis due to climate change, overpopulation, and destruction of the planet's ecosystem. She saw this crisis as the turbulent birth pains of a new era of history, the beginning of a genuinely united global village. I saw it as the beginning of the end, an end suffered by so many species that had also gone extinct in the natural process of evolution for one set of reasons or another. Our discussions, when not about the children, had become flat and short. My sense was that Karen saw me as a kind of curmudgeon. Yet I was still surprised when she announced that she wanted to separate. I hadn't realized the depth of her unhappiness and loneliness in our marriage. I wondered if she had met someone, but I didn't want to ask.

My malaise began before the operation when I realized how alone I was about to become. As much as I knew I couldn't change who I was, I felt the oppressive weight of a failed marriage and the lifelong consequences this would have for our children.

Pancakes: they're easy and fun to make, delicious (especially with walnuts in them), and the kids love them. We prepared dinner together. Rachel makes a good sous-chef, and Ben, a good consumer, particularly when maple syrup is involved. Over dinner, we talked about their day at school. Rachel is in grade one, and Ben is in pre-kindergarten.

After dinner, we played a game of Chutes and Ladders. Rachel won, her self-satisfaction gleeful. Then Ben wanted to put on his new Spiderman costume and wrestle, but I wasn't ready yet so soon after my operation. Nevertheless, wanting to at least see him in his new outfit, I helped him put it on. His second Spiderman costume, it was a tighter fit that looked better on him than the first. He demonstrated superb Spiderman skills while Rachel worked on a jigsaw puzzle. Her skills at this were exceptional and she regularly completed puzzles for kids three or four years older than her.

Finally came the ritual bath and brushing of teeth, and story time. This night the kids wanted to tell *me* stories, yarns they'd invent as they were telling them. First Rachel told a story about dinosaurs and two children, using a dinosaur picture book as a storyboard. Full of twists and turns, it revealed her dramatic imagination. Ben followed Rachel with a dinosaur story too. Except for the part about Rex the Tyrranosaurus rex, his cherished stuffed animal and by now practically a family member, his story made little sense, but was still delightful.

Curiously, both children became almost obsessed with dinosaurs at the same time. I wouldn't have expected this from a girl, yet both could tell me more about dinosaurs than could most of my graduate students who were pursuing advanced degrees in evolution theory. Ben, a precocious tyke with a big sister to mentor him, can name every dinosaur with near-perfect pronunciation. His audiobooks have also taught him well. The instant you put your finger on the picture he can specify the dinosaur: "Brachiosaurus!" "Ankliosaurus!" "Pteranodon!" "Corythosaurus!"

This night Rachel asked a question scientists have been studying for decades: "What happened to the dinosaurs?" It's a good question, and one that makes any student of evolution uneasy. I tried to give an answer that was age-appropriate. Long before humans existed, millions of years ago, the dinosaurs ruled the Earth. They were the world's greatest creatures. This was called the Age of Reptiles. Everything that is alive changes. The Earth lives, too, and it changed. It became a place where the dinosaurs could no longer live. They disappeared, and all we have left of them today are their bones. A new age then came, the one we live in now. Today, humans rule the Earth.

"How did the Earth change?" Rachel asked.

I had to be careful how much I explained: The climate changed. The plants that dinosaurs ate disappeared. They ran out of food.

I was grateful that Rachel seemed satisfied with the answer and soon drifted off to sleep. Ben was already asleep. Any explanation more than this might have caused nightmares. Contemplating the demise of the dinosaurs can lead only to dismal conclusions, even for adults. Think about it. Sixty-five million years ago there occurred a mass extinction that killed off seventy percent of the Earth's species, including the dinosaurs. This marked the shift from the Mesozoic Era, or Age of Reptiles, to the Cenozoic Era or Age of Mammals. Of the numerous theories to explain this, two are prevalent, and they are both cataclysmic. The first theory is that a huge asteroid or meteorite hit the Earth—possibly in the Yucatan—and the second is that there was a massive volcanic eruption. Either of these would have caused dramatic climate changes, such as extreme atmospheric cooling alternating with heating; months or years of darkness due to dust and soot; acid rain; and the greenhouse effect. All this would have adversely affected the Earth's plant life and food supply.

The demise of the dinosaurs was not exceptional. There have been at least five mass extinctions. The one involving the dinosaurs, the end-Cretaceous extinction, wasn't even the biggest. The end-Permian extinction, occurring some 200 million years earlier, killed ninety percent of the Earth's species. In the course of evolution, probably less than five percent of all species that ever lived are still alive today. In other words, it is the fate of most species to go extinct. Many scientists believe that we are today threatened by a new, sixth mass extinction due to the combined effects of habitat destruction, invasive species, pollution, human overpopulation and overconsumption, and climate change. They call it the Holocene or Anthropocene extinction. Thousands of species have already disappeared. What makes us think we can weather such environmental trauma better than the dinosaurs? These sturdy giants had ruled the Earth for over 150 million years. Compare this to the mere 200,000 years our species, *Homo sapiens*, has been on the scene. If current trends continue, our global ecosystem may once again collapse, requiring a long period for recovery. It would not necessarily be the first time humans played a role in widespread extinction. Scientific studies suggest that when humans first reached Australia about 50,000 years ago, they set massive fires—possibly to clear the land—that led to the extinction of at least sixty species of mammals and birds. But aren't such episodes a part of the evolutionary process too? After all, do our own destructive impulses belong to a different order than nature's?

Watching my children sleep gave me relief from these thoughts. For a brief moment, the recklessness of nature and humanity was shut out. But as always, it would be too brief.

After the kids had fallen asleep I made myself a cup of tea. My ambivalence about consulting Gellert resurfaced, and became more clear. I felt apprehensive about the huge gulf between the evolutionary psychology I had, after years of study, come to appreciate as the foundation of human nature, and the psychology I was now turning to in order to examine my anesthesia experience. Evolutionary psychology incorporates the findings of evolutionary biology, zoology, ethology, anthropology, and social and cognitive psychology. There is not a single field of human behavior or activity that it cannot shed light upon. Romantic love, humor, play, gossip, morality, altruism, nationalism, war, and even genocide can be understood as means to enhance our survival. Of course, this is not to say that evolutionary psychology condones our aggression; it merely explains it.

Deciding to see Gellert was a huge departure from my way of thinking, and I was suspicious of the outcome and where it would lead. Did he practice the scientific method, with its emphasis on hard evidence, or was his approach to problem-solving based on fanciful intuitions and wishful thinking? I was especially uncomfortable with his particular leanings toward the unconscious mind—the so-called "depth" that his school of psychology believes lies beneath the waking mind or ego. Evolutionary psychology approaches the unconscious primarily as a process of brain activity, acknowledging that most of what goes on in the human organism in service to its survival, such as breathing and digestion, goes on unconsciously. Depth psychology, as it is known, is more interested in the contents of the unconscious—dreams, repressed emotions, psychological complexes, and so on. Evolutionary psychology would agree with Freud that dreams function as vents that let out the pressures of the mind at night, and thus serve an adaptive purpose. And it might even agree with Alfred Adler—another depth psychologist who like Carl Jung was originally a student of Freud's—that they represent insecurities, inferiorities, and other problems that the unconscious is trying to solve. This too is obviously adaptive. But that dreams have profound meanings like the kind Jung talked about, that they have a knowledge and purpose beyond the ego's and are guiding the ego toward wisdom, or that they can predict the future—that is something more in line with primitive and ancient views of dreams as divine revelations.

Why was I turning to Gellert—a Jungian who valued such magical thinking more than modern science—to help me make sense of a bizarre experience that needed a modern sensibility and intellectual approach to decipher it? I had to be careful with my choices. My grip on reality was tentative and in question. I was in a state of internal chaos and confusion. Before this experience, I was certain I am an animal at the mercy of the immutable laws of nature and with no different a fate than all other animals. I was certain that nothingness follows death and that life is only as meaningful as we make it. But just as certainly, Gellert would want me to descend into the abyss of irrational thinking, as if I weren't already disturbed enough by my anesthesia experience. I could only wonder, was that really wise? I would have to relive it all over again.

First Installment
This Must Be a Hallucination

I open my eyes and see tall blades of grass. I am on my back, my head to one side. I run my hand along my body from my waist up to my head and scalp. I have no hair on my head. I touch my face.

Barefoot and in a hospital gown, I slowly stand up. I am standing on a patch of grass in the trough of a sloping forest canyon. Beside me is a well-worn trail that snakes down along the canyon floor and twists out of sight. Above me the trail continues, but I can't see where.

A warm, balmy breeze blows into the opening of the back of my gown. *How did I get here?* I scroll my memory to see if I can find a clue, but to no avail. I remember *nothing*. Absolutely nothing. I don't know who I am, I don't know my name, I don't know where I come from. I don't know anything.

There is movement far below. Somebody is coming. Minutes pass as I try to figure out what to do. What *can* I do? I can hide, but then what?

A man comes into view about two hundred yards from me. He is about six feet tall with dark features. His T-shirt reveals an athletic build.

"Are you Richard Caldwell?" he shouts.

Yes, that's who I am! I am Richard Caldwell who a moment ago was about to go into the operating room for surgery. I was just injected with a sedative. How did I get from there to here?

"I'm Marc Daniels," he says as he reaches me. He is cordial, but not particularly friendly. He eyes me from head to toe. "Are you alright?"

"I don't know," I say. "I think I'm supposed to be in the hospital."

He stares at me.

"How do you know who I am?" I say.

"My godfather sent me to get you. He lives on top of the mountain that this canyon leads to."

He pulls out a cell phone from his pocket and presses a few buttons. I wonder how he is going to get reception here. There are no signs of civilization around.

"Hi honey. How are you?" he says into the phone. "Our guest has come from a hospital. All he has got on is a hospital gown. Can you get him some clothes?"

He listens to the other party.

"He's about my size, a couple of inches shorter," he responds, and then listens again. Turning to me, he says, "What's your shoe size?"

"Nine and a half," I say automatically, surprised that I know this about myself but, evidently, little else.

"Nine and a half," he repeats into the phone.

Again a brief delay, and he says, "Okay sweetie, meet you there."

And he shuts off the phone and puts it back into his pocket.

"The trail has stones. Can you manage?" he asks.

"I think so."

"Good. We have to get there before sunset."

He walks some fifteen yards ahead while I stand still. "Are you coming?" he shouts after stopping and turning to face me.

I follow.

The trail is a steady climb upwards. Lush, green shrubbery flanks both sides of it.

"Do you know how I got here?" I ask Daniels.

He stops abruptly, turns around, and says, "This will sound strange to you, but if you came from a hospital you are still in it. You are here in mind. Not *your* mind, but mind. You must have been in a state that allowed you to cross the threshold between your world and this one."

Taking his words into *my* mind, which I *know* is sane—even though I can remember hardly anything before this moment—I analyze them. *Your world and this one?* That is nonsense. There is only one world. It becomes instantly clear. There is no other possible conclusion. If I was injected with a sedative in preparation for surgery, *this must be a hallucination.* Something must have gone wrong with the anesthesia. Yet how strange: this place seems physically real, and my body has sensation. He, too, seems physically real.

Problem: if I treat this hallucination as real, I'm feeding it. What should I do? I don't seem to have much choice but to play along. But at all costs I must keep my wits about me.

"Who is your godfather?" I ask after we've covered some distance.

"You'll see."

"What does he want with me?"

"You'll see that too."

"Whom were you talking to?"

"My wife."

"Where did you come from just now?"

"The foot of the canyon. We're approaching the south face of the mountain. My wife will come from the other side. You keep falling behind. Are your feet bothering you?"

"Yes. And it's hard to move in this gown."

He stops again and faces me.

"Take it off," he says.

"What!?"

"Take it off and turn it around and tie it in the front. You've got your butt hanging out through the slit and you can't move your legs this way."

I take it off. As I'm preparing to put it on with the opening in the front he grabs it from my hands and rips it down the middle.

"*What are you doing!?*" I exclaim.

"Here. Take each half and wrap it around each foot as a shoe. You need to be able to walk."

"I'm naked!"

"Yes, and you're no beauty either. Come on. Let's go."

I make "shoes," tying the ends of the rags together. This hallucination is bewildering and banal at the same time.

As we climb quietly, I wonder what could have gone wrong in the surgery. If I'm in a medically induced state of mind, it should end when the anaesthesia wears off. But when will that be?

Again I try some conversation. "The last thing I recall I was preparing for surgery. I was being sedated. What do you know about that?"

"Nothing. People come here in different ways. Drugs are not uncommon."

"I wasn't taking that kind of drug. This shouldn't be happening."

"People also come during a close encounter with death. Maybe you came that way."

"Where exactly are we?"

Stopping momentarily, he turns toward me. "We are in France."

He then resumes climbing. I think of the *Saturday Night Live* sketch with Dan Ackroyd playing the father of a family of alien Coneheads visiting Earth and posing as French people. Why can I remember that and little else? If I weren't so confused and vulnerable I would laugh.

"Why France?" I ask, struggling to keep up with him.

"This is where my godfather is from. He lived in New York at the time he died, but he is originally French."

"*At the time he died?* What are you talking about!?"

"You are in a land where the laws of your world are no longer fixed in the ways familiar to you. This is where the things you know and see in your world live in their essential forms, and continue to live when they are no longer alive in your world."

We come to the base of a small mountain and begin to ascend on the same trail. This mountain is real. The hot sun is real, too.

The terrain is rough but picturesque, and the foliage full and northerly—I imagine, like the foothills of the French Alps—yet I'm in no frame of mind to enjoy them.

"If your godfather died and is alive here," I say, "is this the afterlife?"

"It's a parallel universe, to be more precise," Daniels responds. "Don't try to make sense of it the way you make sense of the world you come from."

Physics is of course nowhere near proving the existence of parallel universes, but it has hypothesized *how* they might exist. I don't know how I know that, but evidently, I do. It appears as if this hallucination is constructing this narrative with information I am familiar with, information already in my mind.

"If I was brought here to meet your godfather," I say, "why wasn't I brought directly to him? Why is this mountain hike necessary?"

I am looking for loopholes in the narrative.

"The doorway between universes is a complicated phenomenon," Daniels says. "You weren't beamed here according to precise coordinates, like on *Star Trek*. We're fortunate to have found you within walking distance."

"Where are the people in this universe?"

He stops and turns around again, moves his eyes down and up my body, and says, "You want to be around people?"

I don't like this Marc Daniels. He is not only aggressive but sarcastic.

After some more climbing, I ask if he lives with his godfather.

"No," he says. "I live nearby. I visit him regularly, cook him a dinner and talk. My wife likes to come—she has become an admirer of his."

"You're American, aren't you?" I say.

"I was born here and went to America when I was eight."

As we continue to ascend, I return to my medical predicament. Could this be a post-operative state? Steroids administered often after surgery to reduce swelling are known to have hallucinogenic effects in sufficient quantities.

Eventually we come to the crest of the mountain and walk along it. In the distance I see signs of civilization and a road that comes up the north side. We come to an opening more or less at the peak, and I see an elegant, stone Tudor house with a chimney a couple of hundred feet ahead.

A woman's voice calls out, "Marc, I'm over here."

To my right I see an attractive woman with a long colorful skirt, high-heeled boots, a small knapsack over her back, and a large paper bag in her hand. Evidently having just arrived herself, she comes over to us and greets Daniels affectionately. She looks me over quickly. I feel like a fool, naked with my feet in big bandages. Our eyes meet. Mona Lisa could envy her enigmatic smile.

First Appointment
What Einstein Saw Inside His Head

As Gellert requested, I emailed him the first installment in advance of our meeting so he'd have time to
review it. I felt apprehension about how he might react.
This feeling followed me into his office on the day of
the appointment. After exchanging greetings and settling
into our seats, he waited for me to begin.

"So what do you think about what I wrote?" I asked
him.

"I'll reserve judgment till I've read more. What do *you*
think?" he asked in return.

"I think the brain is capable of producing almost any
kind of mental state depending on how it is stimulated."

"I agree," he said. "Do you have any idea how your
brain might have been stimulated?"

"I could take a guess at which parts were stimulated
and which anesthetized, but as to why it happened, I
have no idea. I asked my surgeon about my experience a
couple of weeks later, without giving him the details, and
as I indicated when you and I first met, he thought it was
a hallucination I had after coming out of the pentobarbital coma. But that's not the case, Michael. I know that.
I was able to recollect the entire experience shortly after

awakening, and, in fact, although I was confused about whether the surgery had already taken place, I wasn't delirious."

"Have you done any research on this?"

"Some," I said. "I read that hallucinations can occur not only when one is coming out of anesthesia but when going under it. A state of delirium can be experienced while the anesthesia is taking effect, but once it does, the brain should be completely inactive. That's why there are no dreams during anesthesia and absolutely no sense of time passing, as we sometimes have even when sleeping. I did read one study that claimed that one percent of patients undergoing general anesthesia reported awareness. Two percent reported hallucinations and eight percent reported dreams. What do you know about this sort of thing?"

"Not much. I have a colleague who was certain she was wide awake throughout her open-heart surgery. She believed something went awry in the administration of the anesthesia. She couldn't open her eyes or move her body, but she said she was fully alert through the whole procedure."

"That sounds horrible."

"She made that abundantly clear, too. Tell me, I'm interested in your state of mind before the surgery."

"I was in a state of shock, I suppose. Numb. I had so little time to prepare for the surgery that I could only attend to the most immediate and practical concerns. The day before the operation I had already been admitted to the hospital and was under special care in the emergency unit. Karen came in as soon as I called her. I spent much of the day preparing and notarizing the documents that gave Karen power of attorney over all health and financial decisions should I not be able to make them myself. I informed my department chairperson that I would be out for at least eight weeks, and together we figured out who should pick up my courses for the remainder of the semester. I also made plans with my brother to fly in after the operation to help out. Toward the end of the day they shaved my head and took a supply of my blood in case I should need it during the surgery."

"What about the kids?"

"Karen said she'd explain everything to them in a simple and reassuring way. She made arrangements for friends to take care of them overnight so she'd be free to come to the hospital early the next morning for when the operation was scheduled."

"And how was it between you and Karen?"

"We didn't have much privacy or quality time, but managed to share a few words. She shared her grief around her decision to separate. I tried to reassure her that everything would work out alright."

"How were you feeling about her?"

"Remorseful about the separation, but in a way, I was glad the health crisis came after the separation. I wouldn't want her to stay with me just because she felt obligated to. I also felt concern for her. If anything should happen to me, she'd have to carry the lion's share of everything with the kids. And of course, I was grateful for her being there."

"What was your state of mind particularly the night before the operation?"

"Fearful, but hopeful. The doctor was optimistic."

"Did you sleep?"

"Curiously, I had little trouble falling asleep. I was

really tired. They also gave me something to dull the pain of the headache."

"Do you remember any dreams that night?"

"No."

"What happened in the morning?"

"I was up by 5:30 to prepare for the operation. Karen arrived soon after. They wheeled me into a room that had other patients also preparing for surgery. Karen was with me the whole time."

"What was your state of mind then?"

"Resigned. I really wasn't very nervous. I knew if I didn't get this thing in my head fixed, I would surely die. The only thing that scared me more than the surgery or even dying was the prospect of brain damage. After all, I'm a man whose identity depends upon the life of the mind."

"What do you remember immediately before the operation?"

"A nurse came and administered the intravenous sedative that precedes the general anesthesia. One moment I was awake and alert, and the next thing I know I'm in that canyon on my back. In hindsight, it seemed instantaneous. Of course, hours could have gone by before the hallucination began. Where are you going with all this, Michael?" I was getting impatient with Gellert's questions which had to do with routine preparations for the surgery and not the hallucination itself.

"I'm trying to get a sense if there was a connection between your experience and anything immediately prior to it," he said.

"I don't think there was anything out of the ordinary."

"Then let's turn to the experience itself. Tell me about your state of mind in this portion you wrote about."

I told him how wide awake I felt throughout the event, how physically solid and real the world felt. He asked if that physical sense felt the same to me in dreams. I told him it was much more vivid, and also that I couldn't wake myself up. No matter how hard I tried, I couldn't break out of the state I was in. I explained that in dreams I usually don't have an awareness that I'm dreaming. Here I kept questioning my own state as if I were wide awake. My thoughts weren't just "happening" to me. I could exercise directed thinking. He said that this could happen in dreams too, and that in some cultures this is cultivated as a spiritual art. It's called lucid dreaming.

"So you think this was a kind of dream?" I asked.

"Perhaps. It depends on how you define dreams."

"What kind of dream is so vivid and real that it is indistinguishable from the physical world?"

"A vision. A vision is a waking dream. It often has a stronger energy, thus breaking into consciousness while we are awake. Because of this, it can be even more lucid and physical than dreams, blending in with and using the physical environment. It is not just an image projected out by the psyche the way the projector in a movie theater projects an image onto a flat screen. It is experienced dimensionally. But ultimately it comes from the same place that dreams do. You could say that a vision is a dream that occurs while the body or brain is not asleep."

"But I *was* asleep. I was under deep anesthesia."

"Your mind evidently wasn't."

"What about the content of the hallucination? What do you think of that?" I was again getting impatient with Gellert. I wanted to hear his views on this.

"Why are you so sure it was a hallucination?" he said.

I knew we were now getting to the heart of the matter, to the critical question of whether he could help me or not. He said he'd reserve judgment until he heard everything, but if he actually believed that my experience was in any way "real," I would have gotten up and walked out of his office.

"Aren't all visions and dreams essentially hallucinations?" I asked.

Gellert stared at me. He knew I was baiting him.

"The question revolves around meaning and coherence," he said. "There are illusions with meaningful coherence and illusions with little or nothing coherent about them other than their sensory data and the body and brain phenomena—the urges—that give rise to them. A hallucination is like a thirsty man in the hot desert seeing the mirage of an oasis with a waterfall. It's an illusion driven by his thirst. A vision is more like what Einstein saw inside his head with his famous thought experiment."

I was familiar with Einstein's thought experiments from my readings. The one Gellert was most likely referring to occurred one evening while Einstein was riding a streetcar near the clock tower in the center of Bern, Switzerland. He looked at the tower and imagined the streetcar racing away from it at the speed of light. Because the image of the clock would be traveling at the velocity of the light beam carrying it, he intuited that the clock would appear to have stopped since its image could not catch up to the streetcar. However, his own watch would continue to keep time normally. Then it suddenly struck him that what he imagined was not only about the image of the clock but also about time itself, that it beats at different rates depending on your velocity. In other words, he realized that time was relative. Six weeks later he completed his groundbreaking paper on the special theory of relativity.

"Now that was an illusion that altered the course of history," Gellert said. "You see, a vision has a will of its own as much as a hallucination, yet it's about something real, something meaningfully coherent, even though it can only be imagined. That's why Einstein said imagination is the most important tool for scientific discovery. He was a visionary, in every sense of the meaning."

Gellert was clever. He took a widely known event, the kind that every scientist knows happens typically in scientific research, and manipulated it to prove his point.

"Putting aside for the moment the question of whether or not my experience was a hallucination, what do you think about its content ?" I asked, returning to the main issue.

"That depends on what is meaningfully coherent in it, on whether there is a purpose or aim driving the experience forward. Another way to put that is, what does the unconscious want you to see that you don't see?"

"There is something I should tell you," I said. "I know who Marc Daniels is. It came to me suddenly not long after I came out of the coma."

Either Gellert wasn't surprised, or he kept a good poker face.

"He was a guy I knew in graduate school," I continued, "or rather was just acquainted with. He was a student in the drama department, an actor. He was playing the lead role in Bertolt Brecht's *Galileo*. It was put on by his department and there was a campus buzz about it. Karen, whom I was dating at the time, had met him through a friend of hers. He invited us to the final performance and the cast party after. We both loved theater, so we went. Questionable play, but good production. Daniels was a decent actor. That is really about as much as I knew the guy. He is older here than when I knew him, about the age he would be today, but it was definitely him."

"How long ago was it that you knew him?," Gellert asked.

"About eleven years."

"You haven't seen him since then?

"Haven't even thought about him."

"Why do you think he appeared in your experience?"

"I don't know. Maybe it has something to do with Karen. I think she had a crush on him. I found him obnoxious, actually—not like he was in the hallucination, but just the way he flirted with Karen."

"And she with him?"

"Yes."

"How did that make you feel?"

"Jealous, naturally. I remember now seeing them across the room laughing, and I could see they were quite engaged with each other. They looked like they were having an interesting conversation."

"What came of it?"

"Nothing. I asked Karen later what they talked about. She said their conversation rambled from topic to topic—Brecht, theater, the Renaissance. Karen was in the English department at the time, working on her doctoral dissertation in Renaissance literature."

"So a guy you were acquainted with in graduate school and who played Galileo and made you jealous of his connection with your wife—now estranged wife— appears in your hallucination, as you call it, and acts in the role of a guide?"

"Yes."

"What could that possibly mean?"

"That's why I'm coming to you."

"Well, let's start with the guy. You've given me your historical associations to him. I'd like to know what comes up for you when you think about him. Okay, you're jealous. What else do you feel about him deep down in your gut?"

"Nothing."

"Look over to your left."

"Why?"

"Just do it."

I complied.

Gellert said, "Now imagine him sitting right beside you looking at you. What do you feel?"

"To be honest with you, I want to smash my fist into his face. I feel violent toward him."

I looked back at Gellert. He told me to keep my gaze at him.

"That's a strong impulse," Gellert said. "What irks you about him besides the fact that he flirted with Karen?"

"He seems narcissistic, full of himself. He's smug and self-preoccupied."

"What part of you is like that?"

The question surprised me. Turning to my right, I gestured to an invisible judge, pointed at Gellert, and said in a deep voice, "Your honor, he's leading the witness." I looked at Gellert.

Laughing, he said, "Are you always this funny?"

"I don't know. I seem to have lost my sense of humor."

"Since when?"

"Probably before the operation, when Karen and I separated."

"I have a hunch it was long before that."

"What do you mean?"

"This guy Marc Daniels is also pretty funny. He makes your wife laugh, which makes you jealous, and he's quite humorous here in your story too, even making fun of you," Gellert said, putting his hand on his copy of my account. "So what does he carry for you that you no longer do?"

We sat in silence. Indeed, I thought, Gellert was a master at manipulating the conversation.

"Okay," I said, "let's say Daniels carries my long-lost humor and ability to laugh at myself. What are you getting at?"

"I want *you* to get at it. Let's come back to your gut feelings. Remember, he strips you naked, exposing what's hidden and private."

Gellert's forceful questioning of me itself made me feel naked, exposing what's hidden and private.

"Alright," I said. "If I examine it, I don't like him because I feel both superior and inferior to him. I know

I'm more intelligent than him, but I envy the thing in him that Karen found attractive."

"What is that?"

"He seemed easy-going, a good conversationalist, charming. He was an artist, very colorful. Good-looking, no less. I suppose I feared that Karen might find him more interesting than me."

"So her flirting with him and finding him attractive makes you feel what, in addition to jealous?"

"Threatened."

"What are you insecure about, Richard?"

"I sometimes wonder if I'm good enough for Karen. I worry about having disappointed her—if I've failed to live up to her expectations, and mine."

"But that insecurity goes back at least to when you dated her, if not further. That fist you want to smash into Daniels's face has been clenched for a long time. How come?"

"I don't know."

"Did you fail someone when you were younger?"

I didn't answer.

"What about it, Richard?"

"Nothing out of the ordinary, Michael."

He stared at me again. "Okay," he said.

"Let's return to Daniels," I said. "I think the reason I didn't recognize him was that certain centers of my brain were anesthetized."

"Let's assume that was the case. But let's not assume that this cancels out the psychological significance of your lack of recognition. Perhaps the unconscious designed this experience with full knowledge that you wouldn't recognize him. And regardless, he was *perform-*

ing as a character different from the one you knew eleven years ago, whether as a student or as Galileo. He was altogether unrecognizable."

"That's the part I find really weird—his role in this. I can't figure out what it means."

"Maybe he represents a shadow side of yourself that you just can't recognize."

"Ahh, the famous Jungian 'shadow,'" I said, poking fun at Gellert. He smiled.

"What about it?" he asked. "A guy who is smug and self-preoccupied, but also humorous, colorful, and attractive to your wife. Maybe he is not only the *famous* shadow—the negative shadow—but also the *golden* shadow. This shadow consists of the positive qualities you don't see in yourself or that are underdeveloped, and is often even harder to recognize and integrate than the negative shadow. Daniels seems to carry both."

"Are you saying I'm smug and self-preoccupied? It's the second time you've alluded to that."

"I don't know you well enough to say. It's just a question."

"Are you always so 'in your face' with your patients?"

"I'm sorry you perceive me as being in your face. I was only being direct."

"Okay," I said.

Silence.

"Tell me, what are you feeling right now?" he asked.

I didn't know, but I didn't want to tell him I didn't know. I said nothing.

"Are you hurt by what I said?" he asked.

"No."

"Are you sure?"

"I'm sure."

"Are you angry?"

"Maybe a little."

"Just a little?"

"Just a little."

"Maybe that's not a bad thing."

"Why's that?"

"It gets you out of your head and into your feelings."

We fell into silence again.

Then the son of a bitch said our time is up, as if he wanted me to leave his office stewing.

Second Installment
The Intelligence
of This Hallucination

The three of us are standing in front of the Tudor house.

"I'm Karen," the woman says, introducing herself. She is clearly American, with the hint of a Midwestern accent. Her long, wavy blond hair—highlighted by dark eyebrows and hazel brown eyes that suggest a searching intelligence—glistens in the late afternoon sun. I introduce myself. She pulls off her knapsack and takes some clothes out from it—matching gray sweatshirt and sweatpants, boxer shorts, socks, and a pair of running shoes. All are new. She hands them to me, keeping a good arm's distance from my nakedness. Daniels and Karen talk to each other while I dress.

"What's the matter?" she says as I fumble with the shoes.

"They're Nikes," I say. "They're too small for me in nine and a half. I wear nine and a half in Adidas."

"Well, you didn't say that," Daniels says.

Again I am perplexed by the absurdity of all this.

"They'll be alright," I say, taking the socks off and putting on the shoes without them so my feet would have more room.

When I'm finally ready, Daniels nods towards the house and we start walking towards it. We come to the porch, which has a couple of rocking chairs on it. Daniels knocks on the door, opens it, and announces we are here. We come in to a warmly decorated living room lined with books. The fireplace has a coffee table in front of it on a dark red Persian rug. Two curved-back gold velvet sofas with a small end table and a lamp between them form an L-shape on one side of the fireplace. The other side opens up to a dining room with a large rustic oak table. Behind that appears to be the kitchen, and to the sides are other rooms.

A tall, lean man emerges from one of the side rooms and comes towards us. He is wearing the black shirt and white collar of a priest. He is old, yet emanates vitality. He reaches out to shake my hand and, with a friendly smile and a French accent, says, "*Bonjour*. I am Pierre Teilhard de Chardin."

The name sounds familiar. I should know whose it is, but I can't place it. I struggle to connect it to something—*anything*.

All at once, as if a dam had been broken, a huge block of memory is released, flooding my awareness. *I am an evolutionary psychologist!* I can sense that at least my professional knowledge has become available to me. My relief is immense.

After a few moments, I recognize the name. It has been some time since I've heard it. I take a closer look at the face to see if it's really Teilhard de Chardin's. Long and narrow, with a slightly hooked nose and piercing eyes, it's surely his.

"Please call me Pierre," he adds.

I introduce myself, dumbfounded. *What on earth is going on here?*

My recollections of Teilhard begin to coalesce. A paleontologist in the last century, he played a central role in the discovery of the prehistoric Peking Man (or *Homo erectus pekinensis*) in China around 1930. In the annals of evolutionary science, he is acknowledged more for this than the mystical philosophy which later made him famous—famous mostly to intellectuals in the liberal arts and humanities. Indeed, his effort to integrate the theory of evolution with the biblical idea of creation as an act of God is scorned in scientific circles. The notion that evolution is unfolding according to a divine plan is simply unacceptable to the scientific community because there is no evidence for it. This view also led to Teilhard's censorship by the Catholic Church, which could not reconcile these disparate ideas. He was—is—a Jesuit.

"I know who you are," Teilhard says. "I have read your book." (He must be referring to my recent publication, *How Our Lizard Brain Hijacks Us: The Psychology of Institutionalized Fear*. It examines how the human brain's reptilian core, in its blind service to adaptation, influences such social institutions as marriage, religion, the stock market, the media, and government, including not only divine monarchy and fascism but also democracy.) "When I learned you will be passing by our neighborhood," he adds, "I made special arrangements for you to come by for an early dinner. I hope that is agreeable with you."

"Are you saying I have a choice?" I ask.

"Yes," Daniels says. "You don't have to eat if you don't want to."

Teilhard turns to Daniels.

"Marc," he says, "the professor is only asking natural questions."

Teilhard motions me to sit down on one of the couches in the living room. Marc and Karen go into the kitchen.

"You are not going to be here for very long," Teilhard says to me. "Relax and enjoy yourself. Can I get you something to drink?"

"A glass of water would be nice."

"Marc, would you get him a glass of cold water?"

I am left in the room alone with Teilhard. Daniels comes with a tall glass of water with ice and immediately returns to the kitchen.

"You don't have to worry," Teilhard says. "You are going to be alright. There are complications in your surgery, but in the end you will be fine."

What kind of delusion refers in such a detached, rational manner to the reality it is distorting, acknowledging not only that it exists but commenting on its status?

"How do you know that?" I say.

"That information is already available. Time and space are not what you think they are."

"What are they?"

"In your world, they comprise a four-dimensional block universe, the Einstein-Minkowski model of reality. Here, that universe is one among many that reconfigure the laws of time and space."

"You expect me to believe that?"

"No, I do not. As I said, I have read your book."

"So what is your interest in me?"

"I think you are a very good observer. Your applications of the theory of natural selection and adaptation reveal the intricacies of evolution. I want you to reconsider my ideas in light of recent events in the world. Let them germinate. And see if they can be of any relevance to you."

Oh Mary, Mother of God. Again I wonder what's gone wrong in the surgery. What "complications" is he referring to?

My professional knowledge now restored, I remember that Teilhard had a teleological view of evolution. He believed it has a purpose toward an end, and he envisioned this same purpose similarly at work in the unfolding of the cosmos. He did not fall into the trap of teleology that creationists usually fall into—that the complexity of biological life and the cosmos implies intelligent design and therefore an intelligent designer. He was too well-trained scientifically for that. He knew evolution isn't methodical, but a messy process of instincts and urges groping in the dark. That's why there have been so many maladaptations leading to the extinction of species. His view of the aim of evolution rested upon what he called the "Omega Point"—a term he coined based on the biblical description of Christ as the Alpha and Omega or beginning and end of creation. Teilhard saw human consciousness as the flower that evolution, with all its complexity, diverse species, and dead ends, was from the beginning trying to grow. Evolution aims to increase this consciousness to the point—the Omega Point—at which humanity will unite with God as a single human-divine Being, a phenomenon first embodied in the person of Jesus Christ. The Omega Point is the ultimate destination of human evolution. Basically, Teilhard "Christified" evolution by making it the manifestation of Christ and by making the cosmos the body of Christ. The Church silenced him for his pantheism and other views, and scientists reviled him for his mysticism and teleology.

"Would you like some cheese?" Daniels says as he comes into the room with little toast biscuits and an assortment of cheeses on a plate—camembert, Roquefort, brie.

"Would you like some wine with it, or perhaps something a little stronger?" Teilhard says.

"It won't affect my surgery?" I ask.

"Not at all."

I could use a drink.

"Maybe something a little stronger," I say.

He goes over to a liquor table at one corner of the room, reaches for a dark green, flask-shaped bottle with an elongated neck, and fills two small brandy glasses. The bottle has a label with a gold cross in a red circle, but I can't read the writing. I imagine it may be something from a Catholic monastery.

I look over toward the kitchen to see what the noise is about. Daniels is removing some pots and pans hanging over the island in the middle of the kitchen while Karen is chopping food on its wood counter. Both are wearing aprons. Their back-and-forth rapport punctuated with laughter is that of two people enjoyably working together. Teilhard returns with the glasses and hands me mine.

"*À votre santé,*" he says.

"*À la votre,*" I say, taking a sip. It's tasty. "What is this?"

"Unicum," he says.

"What's that?"

"It's comes from unicorns!" Daniels shouts from the kitchen. "It's made from their semen." He and Karen laugh. Teilhard doesn't seem to get the joke.

"Don't worry," Karen says. "We're not in that kind of magical place. It's a Hungarian herb liqueur. The Hungarians drink it both as an aperitif and a digestif."

"What kind of magical place *are* we in?" I say to Teilhard.

"We are in a Platonic realm, a Tibetan Buddhist bardo, a metaphysical plane, a parallel universe, an astral world—call it what you wish," he says. "We are in a dimension of rarefied thought and images. Not pure thought and images, otherwise there would be no corporeality—no substance—whatsoever. The forms in this realm have density but are incorruptible. They do not decay or die. Pure thought and images, those truly beyond any material form, belong to other realms. Here your body is *subtle*. You actually always have had a subtle body—it exists along with the physical one—but you do not recognize it because you are not used to inhabiting it without the physical one."

I am struck by the intelligence of this hallucination. The ideas Teilhard is raising, bridging from ancient Greek and Eastern metaphysics to the concept of parallel universes in modern physics, are well-known. Whether one believes in them or not, they cannot be dismissed as if they were just made up by my imagination. But again, this delusion could include ideas that my mind is already familiar with from my past, using my own knowledge against me.

"What proof do I have that you are not a hallucination?" I ask.

"What proof do you need? You are here, aren't you?"

"I could be here in a hallucination, too."

"That's true. You want physical proof, don't you?"

"Scientific proof, to be more precise."

"Yes, but you mean proof that can be explained by physical laws and corroborated by physical, empirical experiments. Evidence, no?"

"Yes."

"Supposing you got it, what would you do with it?"

"What do you mean?"

"Would you boldly proclaim that something exists beyond the physical world, or would you come up with some other explanation that proves the opposite is true?"

A strong garlic aroma comes from the kitchen. It smells wonderful. *I am hungry.*

Second Appointment
Smoke That Rises to Heaven

I was eager to see Gellert and get his reactions to the most recent material I emailed him. I wondered what he would think about someone as famous and controversial as Teilhard appearing in my hallucination. Also piquing my curiosity, why was my wife married to Daniels, and why didn't I recognize her too? I decided to start our session with my questions about her since my last installment also began with her.

"As I'm sure you've surmised," I said to him after greeting him, "I didn't recognize Karen, either."

"What do you make of that?" he said.

"It seems that certain memories were blocked, as if I were in a partial amnesia. Parts of my brain, perhaps, were more anesthetized than others. Thus was I able to recover my professional identity and theoretical knowledge, while personal experiences, such as my history with Karen, were lost in oblivion. Yet there must have been some core memory of her for my mind to manufacture her in the hallucination. The same with Daniels."

"And what do you make of this omission?"

"I don't know. You said I didn't recognize Daniels because he might represent something unconscious on my part. Do you think that's the case regarding Karen too?"

"Possibly. Let's say you did recognize her? How would that have affected you?"

"It would have been upsetting. I doubt I could have concentrated on anything else. After all, why is she married to another man, and particularly this man?"

"Good question. Answer it."

"I've been wondering if Karen has been having an affair."

"Have you asked her?"

"No. I don't really want to know."

"Why not?"

"It would only confirm that she no longer loves me, or at least that she no longer wants me as her husband or partner. I admit I've been avoiding dealing with that. Probably that's what has led to the situation we're in now. When she announced some months ago that she wanted a divorce, I was stung by how drastic a measure it was. She agreed instead to a trial separation period, though questioned what would change simply because I moved out. Neither of us realized what a trial it would be, with my brain surgery coming so suddenly."

Gellert asked what led to this request on Karen's part. I explained how we had drifted apart and developed different interests. He seemed particularly interested in her religious awakening, and then turned to my thoughts and feelings about it. "What is it specifically about her interests that you cannot relate to?" he asked.

"They seem to me based on an unexamined faith in things having some purpose, some meaning inherently connected to our growth. I agree that every trial and tribulation in life affords us an opportunity to grow, but for her this had become a religious conviction—a belief that this is why we were put on Earth. To me, we weren't put here for any reason. We're an accident of nature—a miraculous accident, but an accident. We create the reasons for which we live."

"Why is this a problem? There are many happily married couples who tolerate each other's different religious or philosophical views."

"I agree with you. I'm not the one who wanted a divorce."

"What does she say?"

"She says that I have my own religion, without knowing it, and it permeates my approach to everything. She calls it my religion of survival and adaptation, and says it colors all my views and feelings about life, like a pair of invisible sunglasses I don't know I'm wearing. She claims this religion of mine shapes my politics, how I see the world, how I see *myself* in the world. She says I'm pessimistic and one-dimensional. Even with the children, when I read them stories and they ask questions, she says I answer with a survival-and-adaptation slant that robs the story of its magic. She tells me I'm a good father but she doesn't like the message I give the kids about life and the way to live in this world."

"What do you think of that?"

"I'm a realist, Michael. I see no evidence to justify a faith in things unseen and to believe in a divine power that mysteriously guides us in our lives. If Karen wants to believe in God and live a spiritual life, I don't have a problem with that. I just don't want it defining how I live my life and make my decisions. Our differences became more apparent as the kids got older. She wanted to send them to a Waldorf school, I didn't—things like that. I wasn't crazy about the different churches and temples and religious events she was taking them to, the things she was telling them. Religion became a source of contention in our marriage. I wanted my kids to grow up with a sound education, not superstition."

"What are your feelings towards Karen?"

"I still love her. I always thought we would spend our lives together."

"What do you love about her?"

"She's a fine person. She's intelligent, curious about everything. She has strong values and is a very ethical person. She's a great mother. Her zest for life makes living with her interesting."

"What connects you to her?"

I described how we had always enjoyed similar cultural interests—film, theater, museums. Though we were of course in very different intellectual fields, we had always been interested in each other's endeavors. We most connected to each other through outdoor activities. We loved camping, hiking, biking, skiing. We took cross-country trips, camping in national parks. We both loved nature.

In a moment of reflection, I thought about how we now do—or did—these activities with the kids, how I have so many fond memories of our family adventures. One of them flashed before me, when we were camping near a river and while fishing Rachel said something about the rapids. Ben, looking all around excitedly, said, "Where are the rabbits!?"

"So what would it take to get this marriage back on track?" Gellert said.

"I don't know. I guess I really don't get what she feels is missing, and why it's so important to her."

"Maybe Daniels knows. He seems happily married to her. How did you describe them? Two people in the kitchen laughing and working enjoyably together?"

Gellert and I stared at each other.

"You asked me to tell you my dreams," I said after some moments. "I had one last night. It was very disturbing."

"What was it?"

"I wasn't really in the dream, but observing it from an objective vantage point. It begins with a cattle car crowded with emaciated people in tattered clothes. The next thing I see is that they are disembarked at some receiving station. German soldiers, flanked on their sides by other soldiers with guns, tell them to go into a room and take off their clothes so they can shower. I realize then that they're at Auschwitz, or some other Nazi death camp. They don't seem to recognize what's going on. They undress and go into this room. The door is bolted behind them. Pellets drop from a chute in the ceiling. When they hit the floor gas starts coming out from them. People start panicking, clamoring to get out. But at the center of the room there's a group of people who are lifting a girl. She's about eight or nine years old. Three of them are lifting her horizontally above their heads. They are trying to raise her above the gas so that she might survive. But it's no use. The gas is rising. Some of the people start praying. I woke up at that moment, terrified."

Gellert was staring at me again. He then asked if I had any associations.

"Obviously they were Jews," I said.

"What's your experience with Jews?"

"Good ones. I always had Jewish friends, my parents, too."

"Any survivors or children of survivors?"

"In college I dated a girl whose parents were in the camps. I could see how the war had a multigenerational impact. She was born in America but her family life was overshadowed by the effects of the war. Her parents were opposed to her dating me because I wasn't Jewish. We went our own ways eventually, on good terms."

"What are your own associations to Auschwitz?"

"The typical associations anyone might have. It was a horror and tragedy beyond imagination. I doubt my dream captured even a small piece of it."

"What about your family's experience of the war?"

"My father served in the South Pacific. He didn't see any action, though. My mother was a high school student at the time."

"And the girl in the dream?"

"If I think about it, of course my daughter comes to mind. As a father it sends shivers down my spine and makes me sick to the stomach to imagine . . . But in the dream I didn't think of her and the girl didn't resemble her. There's at least a couple of years age difference."

Gellert stared at the floor, as if he were thinking. Turning his gaze back toward me, he said, "What happened to you when you were eight or nine?"

Pausing, I looked at the floor now.

"My sister was killed in a bicycle accident. A truck ran her over. It was the defining event of my childhood."

"I'm very sorry, Richard. That must have been terrible . . . Tell me about it."

"We were living in Chicago at the time. My father was a professor at the University of Chicago. She went out one afternoon on her bike to get some groceries my mother wanted. On the way back a truck veered out of control. She died instantly. My mother fell apart. She was never quite the same again. For years a dark cloud hung over our house. My parents tried to give my brother and me all we needed, but everything seemed so mechanical, forced. It would be a relief for us as well as them when they sent us off to camp in the summers."

"Tell me about your sister."

"We were close. She was fourteen when it happened. Sometimes my brother, who was twelve, would bully me, and Alison would come to my aid and put an end to it. I remember when we were younger she patiently taught me how to play cat's cradle. She was a good kid. I think she may have been my parents' favorite, or at least that's how it felt after she died. Her absence and my parents' silence about her, if anything, made her larger than life."

"How did that affect your experience growing up?"

"I think it made me believe that I had to behave like a really good kid, that I had to get only top grades and should never let loose or make mistakes. This was both to live up to Alison's specialness in my parents' eyes and because I didn't want to add to their burden."

"And you still think your insecurity around disappointing your wife is nothing out of the ordinary?"

Gellert's comment stunned me. He waited me for me to absorb it. I didn't know what to say.

"Why do you think you are dreaming this now?" he asked.

"I have no idea."

"What do you imagine the dream wants from you?"

"What do you mean?"

"Dreams come to tell us something, but they also often want something from us, perhaps to recognize some long-lost truth or develop a new attitude about something or settle some unfinished business. One of history's worst tragedies is revealed to you as you watch this desperate effort to save this girl's life. What does the dream want you to understand?"

"I can't connect it to anything, Michael. To me, the Holocaust illustrates human nature's capacity for destruction and evolution's blindness. We have within us impulses that can be turned against ourselves, threatening our own extinction."

"Do you know what the word 'holocaust' literally means?"

"Doesn't it mean 'sacrifice'?"

"Yes, exactly. Literally, it means 'burnt offering.' It's the Greek word for sacrifice by fire. What in you was sacrificed when Alison died?"

I had to think about his question. It was strange to think about my sister's death as a sacrifice on *my* part. *She* was always the one who was lost.

"I suppose a certain innocence and optimism about life," I said. "After that my parents became almost militant atheists. They were already followers of Bertrand Russell. Russell had taught at the University of Chicago before my father got his appointment in the philosophy department there, but his influence was still strongly felt. My parents met him when we all went to England one summer when we were little kids. They admired his sober outlook on life, and of course, his humanitarianism and social activism. You could say we were brought up on Russell's philosophy of logic. Beyond question it influenced not only my interest in science and choice of profession, but also my attitude toward religion. Russell was not only a philosopher of science and mathematics, but an outspoken atheist and critic of Christianity. After Alison died my parents became even more convinced that there could be no God in a universe so randomly cruel. Any talk about God or life after death or religion was met with subtle derision by my father and simple disinterest by my mother. Maybe this is what was sacrificed—an openness to entertain religious questions."

"How do you imagine you might have developed if not for your parents' view on religion?"

"I had a religious curiosity no more or less than any other kid. If anything, Alison was the one in our family most curious about religion. She went with some of the neighborhood kids to church every once in a while. My parents did not stop us from exploring religion, but for sure they didn't encourage us either. Though I hope you're not insinuating that all atheists have some childhood reason for their beliefs."

"Of course not. Belief could be a matter of temperament as well as childhood influences. But in your case I'm wondering. Why does a man who so clearly professes disbelief in religion end up marrying a woman who in this regard turns out to be his opposite, and why does he have a visionary experience involving Teilhard de Chardin, one of the twentieth century's greatest religious figures? And then why a dream about the Holocaust, perhaps the greatest religious event since the Crucifixion?"

"How was the Holocaust a religious event? If anything, it was anti-religious."

"It was anti-religious because it went against religious values and was such an abomination. But it was religious at the same time because it raised the burning question your parents struggled with, how could there be a God in a universe so randomly cruel? It raised the problem of evil to a whole different level. Holocaust theology, a specialty within theology, attempts to answer this question. Curiously, many of its adherents are atheists."

"What are you getting at?"

"The girl in your dream is very likely an image of your soul, what Jung called the 'anima.' I'm suggesting that in some way your young soul was sacrificed when your sister died. That is what a burnt offering essentially is. It turns the goat or whatever is being sacrificed into smoke that rises to heaven. Isn't that what happened to the victims of Auschwitz? The people in the gas chamber of your dream start to pray. This is a religious dream, Richard. I'm wondering if what was sacrificed in your young soul was a religious attitude, and if you are being asked to now develop this."

His interpretation was compelling, but nevertheless, its prescription was beyond my means. "You're suggesting the dream is asking me to believe in God?"

"No. A religious attitude is more about *how* one sees than *what* one sees. There are religious attitudes that are expressly nontheistic, such as Buddhism, many shamanic traditions, and, for that matter, Einstein's view. A religious attitude, as the mystic Meister Eckhart would say, is more about finding our own Godhood than a god above us."

"I don't necessarily have a problem with that, Michael. To me, nature and evolution are divine just as they are. They don't need a God to make them something more. But what about Teilhard? What then is his connection to this?"

"Again, I'd like to reserve judgment till I've read more. I want to hear what he has to say."

Thus concluded our second meeting.

First Interlude
A "Growing Concern"

Amy Kassabian is the director of Rachel's private school. A middle-aged woman, she is a seasoned educator and administrator. Karen and I sat opposite her across her desk in her office. To her side was Roberta Anderson, Rachel's teacher. We were asked to come in to discuss a "growing concern" with Rachel.

After some discussion of my surgery and recuperation, Kassabian turned to the issue at hand. "She's overall a lovely, well-behaved child and an excellent student," she said. "But we've observed that she can at times be indifferent to other children in a way that is off-putting and rude. We thought we should raise this with you and see if you've observed something similar at home."

"Can you give us some examples?" Karen asked.

"In class I sometimes assign group projects," Anderson said. "On more than one occasion a student has for one reason or another been moved from another group into the group Rachel is in. I notice Rachel ignores the student and then gets angry with her for no apparent reason. She says mean things like the student can't participate because it's not really her group or she came late, or she gives no reason at all. When I've asked what she's feeling she shrugs her shoulders. When I've asked specific questions, like if she's angry for some reason, she says no. Last week I took her aside and tried to have a discussion with her about it. She seemed to shrug it off and then it happened again a few days ago. We've observed similar behavior in the school yard. She can be very cliquish and hostile."

"We *have* noticed something similar," Karen said. "Just the other day I was car-pooling some of the kids to school and when one of them got in the car Rachel acted as if she didn't even exist."

"And we saw something like what you've described at her friend's birthday party a couple of weeks ago," I said, looking at Karen. "Remember?"

The four of us probed the possible underlying factors of this recent development, eventually turning again to my surgery and, inevitably, to our separation. Kassabian and Anderson were surprised. It was the first they heard of it. We naturally discussed the emotional effects the separation could be having, and how we were managing it with Rachel—how did we answer her questions, how did she respond to staying in my apartment, have we noticed anything else unusual? We agreed we would have a series of conversations with Rachel, addressing any fears or feelings she might be having as well as her behavior with other kids. We of course would not be recriminatory or blaming, but rather try to help Rachel understand what might be making her reject others. We'd try to help her empathize with how they might feel being rejected. And we would monitor this closely over the next period.

To my mind, Rachel's behaviors reflected typical group dynamics. Newcomers to any established group—

be they immigrants to a country, new employees in a company, or students entering an already formed study group—often must face the defensive but aggressive behaviors of its members. Rejection, elitism, hazing, and even racism are rooted in instincts of self-protection and survival, and though unfair, are natural evolutionary mechanisms. Not so natural is why this mechanism has been triggered now in nonthreatening situations. Is our family the actual group whose protection and survival Rachel is trying to assure?

Third Installment
Turning the Scheme of Evolution on Its Head

D inner is ready," Daniels announces.
"Come," Teilhard says to me, "a feast for the mind that you think is your body."

We go into the dining room. Teilhard and I sit facing each other across the length of the rectangular table. Places are set for Daniels and Karen to our sides. A French baguette is at the center of the table. After Karen sits down, Daniels serves the appetizers. Teilhard registers my uneasiness.

"They are escargots with garlic butter, *very good!*" he says.

"What's your problem?" Daniels chimes in. "If all this is just a hallucination, what difference will it make?"

They all laugh. He has a point.

"Tell me, Richard," Teilhard says, pronouncing my name in a French way. "What do you think is going on in your world today from an evolutionary viewpoint?"

"I must admit I'm not optimistic. I think global warming and pollution are having effects that we will not fully see until later, and I'm afraid, until *too* late to prevent an ecological collapse and mass extinction of many species. Deforestation and desertification might severely impact the delicate balance that maintains the planet's sustainability, not to mention its beauty. The flooding of coastlines caused by the melting ice sheets of the Earth may uproot entire populations, forcing them to migrate elsewhere. Civilization and the course of human evolution may even be dramatically altered."

"A major crisis, unlike any since prehistoric times, *non*?"

"Yes, and I should add that the crisis is not in the future. It's already upon us."

"You described the dangers very concisely," Teilhard said. "Now what would you think if I told you that this crisis affects not only the environment and society, not only the biosphere, but the noosphere, that it is wider and more profound than we even know?"

Noosphere—another idea of Teilhard's that I haven't thought about since first learning of it. Perhaps even more famous than the Omega Point which he sees as evolution's divine goal, it is just as forgettable, at least to me. As I recollect, Teilhard added a third sphere—the noosphere—to the two established spheres of the Earth. The first and oldest sphere of evolution is the actual Earth itself—the geosphere, including the barysphere, lithosphere, hydrosphere, atmosphere, and stratosphere. Over time, the geosphere, whose minerals all life evolved from, gave rise to the second sphere, the biosphere. First there formed microorganisms, cells, and different plant species. Then came all the animals, and finally, humans. But the good Father Teilhard believes that a noosphere, a sphere of the mind, is now emerging out of the biosphere *as an extension of the Earth itself.* This is like a skin or membrane of human consciousness on the surface of the Earth—a "thinking layer," as he described it. It is a metaphysical concept with absolutely no grounding in scientific observation.

"Would you like some wine to wash down the snails?" Daniels interrupts.

"Please," I say.

He then offers Teilhard and Karen wine. He affectionately calls Teilhard "Père Pierre," and is as respectful toward him as he is condescending toward me.

"*Salut,*" Teilhard says, and we all clink our glasses together.

"Father Teilhard," I say, "with all due respect, I don't believe in your noosphere."

"I know, but you should. You are in it right now."

He is actually correct in a manner of speaking. *Noos* in Greek means "mind." Since all this is going on as a hallucination, it *is* in the sphere of my mind. Of course, that is not the way he means it. He means it as a distinct phenomenon and phase of evolution. Nowhere near complete, it is yet to reach its full stride. Connecting all human thought and consciousness on Earth, it would eventually pave humanity's way to the Omega Point, not only unifying all people but also uniting them with God.

"The place you are in now," Teilhard continues, "is a different dimension. I said before that you could call it a Platonic realm, an Aristotelian metaphysical plane, a Tibetan Buddhist bardo, or a Hindu astral world. Such realms are becoming more accessible to ordinary people these days—and not just sages, mystics, and saints, as in the days of old—*because the noosphere is expanding into these dimensions* and making spiritual commerce with them more possible."

Now this expansion of the noosphere into other dimensions is something I do not recall coming across among Teilhard's ideas. But then, when Teilhard developed his ideas, he was not in such a dimension either, as we both allegedly are now. To me these dimensions are simply products of the human imagination—in other words, make-believe fantasies.

Karen asks if everyone is ready for the main course and excuses herself as she goes into the kitchen.

Another burst of fine aroma wafts out of the kitchen as Karen returns with hot mitts on, carrying a casserole dish. Daniels gets up and gets a large bowl of salad and a serving dish with grilled asparagus. I welcome the intrusion to gather my thoughts about how strikingly organized and intricate this hallucination is. Not only is sensorimotor functioning completely realistic and under my control, but so are the higher operations of logical and abstract thought, as observable not only in Teilhard's metaphysical discourse, but in the very fact that I'm thinking this. The limbic system and cerebral cortex govern perception and imagery, while the subcortical limbic structures affect imagery, memory, emotion, motivation, and spatiotemporal cognition. All this shapes one's sense of familiarity and what makes things meaningful and real. When these parts of the brain have been electrically stimulated in experiments, subjects have reported cosmic or otherworldly visions, out-of-body experiences, ecstasy, déjà vu, and similar phenomena. Somehow the surgery or medication must be stimulating these parts of my brain to create this highly detailed and verbally sophisticated—indeed, verbose—hallucination.

"*Bon appétit!*" Teilhard joyfully exclaims. We serve ourselves. The moist quiche Alsacienne with its melted sharp cheddar cheese, golden-brown sautéed onions, and dry-cured, crisp, salty bacon is exquisite. Teilhard, however, is not distracted by it. "So, what do you think this expansion of the noosphere into higher realms has to do with what you described appropriately as the impending danger on Earth?" he asks.

"I don't know," I say. Can it be that the wine is getting to my head? I'm feeling a little intoxicated.

"I will tell you," he says. "The reason more spiritual commerce is becoming possible, the reason the noosphere is expanding into the higher realms, is only partly because of the unifying of humanity's consciousness due to technological innovations like the worldwide web."

I recall how Teilhard believed that technology and industry not only reflect human evolution but help it along. I also remember reading that certain of his followers have equated cyberspace with the noosphere and advocate the Internet as the harbinger of a new global consciousness.

"There is more to it than that," he adds. "A distinct phenomenon is about to take place as the noosphere is beginning to reach the first of a number of critical thresholds in its development."

Karen is listening intently to Teilhard, her eyes revealing her own reverence for him. Her delicate manner of eating is ladylike. She is the most attractive part of this hallucination.

Teilhard continues. "The reason the noosphere is beginning to now go through a profound transformation in its capacities is because it is about to become recognized for what it is. People becoming more conscious of it makes *it* more conscious. And that empowers it. It is a new vision of God. God is no longer going to be Jesus up on a cross, but Christ-Omega, the Omega Point, the noosphere itself in its fully developed condition. Actually, that is what Jesus on the Cross really symbolizes. 'The kingdom of heaven is within you,' he said. 'I am the Alpha and the Omega, the first and the last, the beginning and the end.' People will realize that their consciousness is itself divine, and that its evolution is God unfolding in their everyday lives, in their day-to-day awareness. This will be a great revolution in consciousness, as great if not greater than the birth of consciousness itself eons ago. The turbulence that humankind is now going through, even if it leads to ecological collapse, is part of the metamorphosis that will take place. That is the way of nature and evolution. The caterpillar becomes a butterfly only after an intense struggle to recreate itself in a new form out of the old one. The snake has to arduously shed its skin to grow. What is happening ecologically and socially now in the biosphere is intimately connected to what is happening in the noosphere. Do you understand what I am saying?"

"Yes. You're saying that evolution is moving toward God, and that the evolutionary crisis that humanity is now facing is in fact ushering in a great leap in its consciousness."

"Have some more wine, my friend," Daniels says as he pours me another glass. Is he trying to get me drunk?

"Father Teilhard," I say, "again, I find these ideas unacceptable. You claim that a noosphere is evolving that will connect or deliver us to a transcendent condition, whatever that would be. Everything we know about the cosmos, by contrast, tells us that it will eventually end in either a big freeze or a heat death, returning to a state of entropy and formlessness. 'Not a bang, but a whimper,' the cosmologists say. All that passed in it will amount to nothing. Even well before that, our sun will become so bright that the Earth will become uninhabitable. Your ideas are at odds with these facts."

"Perhaps there is no contradiction between the two views. Why does it have to be one *or* the other, why not both?"

"How could it be both? How could you both exist and not exist at the same time?"

"There is no reason to assume that something in the cosmos cannot escape entropy. That 'something' would be consciousness. Science has offered no explanation for how life could arise from inorganic matter other than its description of chemical processes, and no explanation *at all* for how consciousness could arise from organic matter. Evolution shows that whatever we are evolving into is not predetermined by what we have evolved from. There is something *within* the manifestations of evolution that transcends the mere forms of those manifestations."

"How could evolution survive entropy?"

"Evolution rises upstream against the flow of entropy. Far, far into the future, the noosphere will reach a certain threshold and its consciousness will break away from the physical dimension. This will represent not so much cosmic *evolution* as *involution*. The stuff of the universe, in its

93

highest evolved form of the human mind, will turn in and move towards its innermost animating force—pure consciousness, the Being of God, the Omega. The cosmos will converge into its essence but lose nothing of the human complexity that will have evolved up to this final point."

"You are turning the scheme of evolution on its head. Instead of mind evolving out of matter, you have reversed their order."

"*Mais non!* The primacy of spirit *is* the cosmic order. Science merely discovered matter—what I call tangential energy—first because it is what first manifests to the eye, what first becomes obvious in the scheme of evolution. But science is backing into the phenomenon of nature. It has thus made the mistake of assuming that matter comes first simply because it has discovered it first. It is spirit—what I call radial energy or what Henri Bergson called *élan vital*—that is the hub of the cosmos and its motivating, creative force. Think of it: how could it be otherwise? How could something as complex as consciousness evolve *out* of the stuff of the universe if the drive toward it didn't exist *within* it to begin with?"

I remember Teilhard's theory about two kinds of energy in the cosmos. My mind must be retrieving this, too, from the recesses of my memory, putting it into his mouth and arming him with his own ideas. Even more unnerving, it is becoming apparent that I am arguing with a very intelligent figure of the imagination who can explain his position very logically and to whom no opposing viewpoint is an obstacle. He consumes other views cannibalistically and incorporates them into his own. His logic, however, has a certain ring to it, its method clearly the same as that of Augustine, Anselm, and Thomas Aquinas, giving faith priority over reason. They too started with the assumption that God's existence was as plausible as his nonexistence, and therefore cannot be disproven. Thank goodness I was raised on Russell's philosophy.

I feel the eyes of Daniels and Karen staring at me as I stare at Teilhard.

He continues. "Even from a purely statistical standpoint, how can you be so certain that there cannot evolve a sophisticated, interconnected consciousness that will act in an enlightened and loving way, that in *all* eternity there can never be an Omega that comes into existence *at some point?* Everything about evolution demonstrates that the fundamental law of the universe is that if something is possible, it will be realized. You seem to forget that consciousness is evolving, and like everything that evolves, it seeks greater and greater organized complexity. It is likely that eventually evolution will become conscious of itself. *That* is the phenomenon of both man and the noosphere."

"The Omega you are talking about," I say, "is in the final analysis just a conjecture. What evidence do you have that it will *ever* come into existence? What the Bible tells you?"

"The key element of the Omega," Teilhard replies, "is basically consciousness. Something cannot come out of nothing unless the potential for it existed in the first place. Whatever exists in evolution must have already existed in *some* form or another before evolution, before the Big Bang, and will continue to exist after the end of the universe in the higher form it will then have attained.

This course of evolution is no other than God in a pro-cess of becoming. Theologically speaking, it is the way God incarnates into the cosmos, evolving *himself* from primordial chaos into higher and higher forms that are finally human and what humanity itself will over time become. Though transcendent, God fulfills or completes himself through creation and man."

"I am not able to draw meaningful analogies between science and theology. Aside from how they historically influenced each other, they are completely unrelated."

"Then let's not talk about theology. Let's talk about the future of consciousness based on what we already know about it. Please tell me your working definition of consciousness."

At last, perhaps I can now ground his argument in some hard facts and get the boogeyman out of it.

"Aside from being the state of awareness or awake-ness," I say, "consciousness defies any formal definition, at least so far. From a neuroscientific point of view, it is not a property or operation different from the brain, but is a consequence of the increased complexity of the brain. Evolutionarily speaking, consciousness is an adap-tive function of the brain. That is the simplest way to put it."

"Simple is good, although not always correct or com-plete, as in this instance. In any case, how do you think consciousness began, evolutionarily speaking?"

I proceed to explain that consciousness probably began some 200 million years ago as a result of the evolving cerebral cortex of mammals. Human conscious-ness is the product of a brain that has increased its size at least threefold over the past four million years. Its structure consists of three basic parts—an inner core, a middle wrapping around that core, and an outer wrapping. Though integrally connected in order to perform complex tasks, each part corresponds to a distinct period of our evolution. The inner core is the brain stem and cerebellum, the oldest, reptilian part of our brain— the so-called "lizard brain." Its primitive flight-or-fight fear responses and repetitive behaviors are rigidly programmed to assure safety and survival. The middle wrapping is the limbic system, or paleomammalian, prehistoric part of our brain that regulates our emotions and more complex instincts. And the outer neocortex, or the neomammalian part of the brain, is, with its two hemispheres and capacities for rational thinking and speech, the most recent evolutionary acquisition. All mammals have a neocortex, but human consciousness owes its distinct characteristics to the intricate folding of the human neocortex.

"*C'est excellent,*" Teilhard says. "But aren't you forgetting something?"

"What?"

"Neurons. What about neurons?"

"Naturally," I say, "they go hand-in-hand with the brain's structural development. Consciousness is associated with the high density of neurons in the cortex of the human brain and with the evolution of uniquely organized patterns of neural activity—neurocircuitry. There probably exist certain neural networks that give rise to conscious states. Neuroscientists are searching for these now."

"*Très bien.* Now, what about synapses?"

I wonder what this phantom of my mind is trying to

do. Clearly, he is orchestrating the discussion so that I reach some conclusion that proves or validates his pseudoscientific theory. Daniels and Karen are listening with rapt attention.

"That's a complicated matter," I say. "The brain has a hundred billion neurons. These send impulses to each other—some electrically, some chemically via neurotransmitters—across the gaps between them. These gaps are synapses. What about them?"

"What do they consist of?"

"They don't consist of anything. They're infinitesimal gaps—one-hundredth of a micron."

"Now, imagine the noosphere as a kind of brain, and yourself as a neuron in it with the billions of other people in the world who are also neurons. We are separated by synapses. Consciousness is somehow transmitted across the synapses, connecting all the individual neurons or people into a single entity, the noosphere. What is happening in the world today is a grand synaptic excitation that is evolving both consciousness and the noosphere. What happened in evolution to create consciousness in the brain is happening now on a new level."

"Father Teilhard," I say, "there is a huge difference between the synaptic gaps between the neurons in our brains and the physical distance between you and me right now. Furthermore, the synaptic excitation of neurons involves an electrical or chemical transmission that *leads* to consciousness. It is not a transference of consciousness itself, as you are implying would occur between people. Anyway, who would want to live in a

world where everyone's thoughts are accessible to everyone else? There would be no privacy whatsoever."

"*Mais non.* Firstly, the noosphere will not be a form-
less merging of everyone's minds together, leading
toward less complexity rather than greater. That would
be like the primordial soup that evolution theory tells us
we evolved from, but occurring on a metaphysical rather
than physical level. People's minds will not melt together
into one mind anymore than the books in a library melt
together into one book. The noosphere will be like a living, breathing library with many books in it, all speaking
to each other from various perspectives. It will be a great
but separate mental body nourished by the consciousness of its distinct parts."

I have no idea how to respond to such a fantastical
notion of humanity's future.

"Secondly," Teilhard says, "perhaps the gap both
between our neurons and the consciousness of individuals is not empty as you think. Perhaps it is not a
classical vacuum but a quantum vacuum, full of energy
and activity. Hasn't quantum theory already been used
to help explain relations between synaptic processes and
consciousness? It provides a different understanding of
how things interact, *non?* In fact, you could think of the
noosphere as a unified field of consciousness similar to
the quantum field, or for that matter, the gravitational
and electromagnetic fields."

"But the gravitational and electromagnetic fields," I
say, "can be observed and demonstrated empirically to
exist, and quantum field theory is becoming increasingly fertile in its applications. Your noosphere cannot

be observed, empirically proven, or even studied. It's just an idea."

Daniels bursts into laughter. "Père Pierre, why are you arguing with him?" he says. "Isn't it clear that he is a devout materialist? He has blind faith only in what he can observe and empirically prove."

"What's wrong with that?" I say. "Why should I believe in something I cannot perceive just because someone says it exists? That's dogma, not knowledge."

"Experiencing things for oneself to make up one's own mind is the sign of an independent thinker," Daniels retorts. "But you assume that the proof that something is real is that it can be tested and measured in an experiment. What if it can't be captured under a microscope, neatly defined and classified? Tell me, you seem to be enjoying my soufflé with great relish. Is it also 'just an idea?' Well, the answer, my friend, is, *yes, it is*. Everything here is just an idea. How are you going to test and measure that?"

"Please, please, gentlemen," Karen says. "We are in France. Everything is civil here."

Exasperated by Teilhard's pontificating and now Daniels's assault, I seek relief by turning to Karen. "What do *you* think about all this?" I ask her. She looks at me with her large brown eyes, and again, that enigmatic smile.

100

Third Appointment
A Romantic Notion of
the Unconscious

When Gellert asked me how I was, I told him of my concerns about Rachel. His support was soothing. I said it was probably a good thing that in my altered state I had no family memories, otherwise my fears for my children—would they ever see their father again?—might have been overwhelming.

"Maybe this has something to do with why only my professional identity became accessible to me," I said. "It's mysterious."

"What else do you find mysterious in your experience?" he asked.

"I'm surprised at how bizarre my imagination is," I said. "Karen's appearance I could at least understand, and perhaps even Daniels. But Teilhard? He's the last person I would dream of meeting."

"Why?"

"I have no connection to him whatsoever, other than the fact that he was an evolutionary thinker. But even there, what's the connection? He was a quack. If not for his part in discovering the Peking Man, he shouldn't even be considered a scientist. His ideas were nonsense, and full of metaphysical trickery. There was some talk about him participating in the 1912 Piltdown Man hoax, probably history's greatest archaeological hoax. Teilhard was part of the digging team. I think that the charge of fraud was disproven, but that he twisted evolutionary science to support his theology is a kind of sleight of hand itself."

"Obviously, he is the last person your *ego* would dream of meeting, but your ego did not dream this. Your unconscious did."

"So what mystifies *you*?" I asked.

After a few quiet moments, he said, "Your vision is unlike any I've heard or read about. On the one hand, it's very surreal. You can't recognize people you know but you recognize a person you never met—Teilhard. Or at least you're intellectually familiar with him. On the other hand, the lack of surrealism is almost surreal itself if you consider the extraordinary imagery of most drug-induced visions or altered states induced by sensory or sleep deprivation. Nothing weird happens here. For example, people don't turn into animals as they do in shamanic shape-shifting visions. They behave in more or less ordinary ways, even rationally. In this regard your experience is similar to the visionary accounts of Hindu and Tibetan yogic masters visiting heavenly worlds or astral realms. Their visions can exhibit extraordinary imagery too, but they have a sense of containment and continuity similar to yours. You were contained in an environment that had the same consistency from one moment to the next. In that regard your vision was even less surreal than the average dream that people have every night."

"What does that mean?"

"I don't know."

"And tell me, what do *you* think of Teilhard?" I asked.

"The historical Teilhard, or the one in your vision?"

"Let's start with the historical one."

"What do you imagine I think of him?"

"I think you're probably an admirer."

"Like Karen?"

"Like the Karen in my hallucination. I imagine the real Karen would like him, too, though we never spoke about him and I don't know how well she is acquainted with him."

"So what would it mean to you if I were an admirer?"

"I'd think you were gullible."

"And if I thought he were full of nonsense, like you do, what would that mean to you?"

"I'd think you understand something about the scientific method and its importance."

"And what might that in turn mean to you in terms of our work together?"

"It would mean to me that you understand the principles underlying consciousness and such experiences as mine and not just be focused on their content. You'd take the brain's limbic system more seriously—how it mediates our memories and emotions, how its amygdala and hippocampus networks affect emotional intensity and otherworldly sensations. In other words, you'd have a more scientific approach."

"Meaning, you'd trust me more, right?"

"I suppose."

"You know, you could have consulted a neuropsychologist who'd be better equipped to talk with you about that, but you chose a Jungian analyst. Why?"

"Because I didn't think they'd be able to help me with the bizarre content that I have no way of understanding. However, I don't want to take one *or* the other approach, but *both*."

"You can do both. I have no problem with you consulting a neuropsychologist to explore the physiological dimension of your experience."

"Okay, I'll consider that."

"You seem to have some grievances about me today. What's that about?"

"I don't know, Michael. I'm just frustrated with this whole thing. It's disturbing."

"What in particular is disturbing you?"

I had to pause for a moment to find the right words to answer that, but I could settle only on the ones that came. "I guess it's that I'm not in control."

"Of course. That's understandable. As if the brain surgery weren't enough, this strange event happened to you unexpectedly, you had no choice in the matter, and you were yanked out of your familiar world like a baby forced out of the womb."

Gellert kept his eyes fixed on me as we sat in silence for some time.

"So, what *do* you think about Teilhard?" I asked again.

He laughed. "You're persistent, to be sure. I already told you what I think. I believe he was one of the towering figures of the twentieth century. He was a religious genius."

"Why do you think that?"

"For one thing, since we were just talking about science, he took a significant step toward integrating it with religion. He built a bridge between two great historical opposites. What did Einstein say—'Science without religion is lame, religion without science is blind'? Teilhard gave science legs it didn't have before, and he gave religion eyes it didn't have before. He redefined Christianity—for those who could appreciate it—in a modern way that makes it relevant. But he was ahead of his time. Perhaps Christianity will catch up with him."

"Maybe he was good for religion, but his speculations have done little for science. He masqueraded them as science, but they were more in the ilk of science fiction than science."

"Maybe science has to catch up to him, too."

"I don't think that will ever happen."

"What if science discovered something like the noosphere? This prospect sounds radical now, but so did the notion of relativity before Einstein came along. That wasn't even on the minds of most scientists in his day."

"They're two different things, Michael. Einstein was dealing with the world of physics. Teilhard's propositions are purely metaphysical."

"'Metaphysical' may in the future be looked upon as an old word for a kind of energy that we didn't yet have a way of understanding and measuring. Wasn't atomic energy once misunderstood and immeasurable?"

"So you believe in this noosphere?"

"I believe in the principle that ideas like the noosphere point to. In fact, the noosphere is very close to Jung's concept of the objective psyche or collective unconscious. I'm sure both thinkers would have agreed on the psyche's role in evolution and its evolutionary aim, even if using different language to describe this. It's no accident that Jung was reading Teilhard's *Phenomenon of Man* in the last days of his life while in the process of dying. He said it is a great book."

"So, turning to the Teilhard of my imagination, I suppose you then also believe the part about the interface of the noosphere with other realms and its significance for the current crisis of humanity?"

"I found that intriguing." I wondered if Gellert believed he had experiences with such realms in his Zen training.

"And you take seriously his analogy of neural activity and the noosphere?"

"It's interesting, too."

Unaware of it, I drifted off into my thoughts. When I returned to the conversation, I saw Gellert looking at me inquisitively.

"I'm just wondering if all this effort we're making is in vain," I said. "What if there's nothing to be gained from it? What if it's nothing more than just a big hallucinatory flight of fantasy?"

"That was no hallucinatory flight of fantasy, Richard. That was a vision. When a figure like Teilhard de Chardin appears in the way he did, conveying a distinct transpersonal perspective, it suggests that this is not a distortion caused by brain dysfunction—or at least it is not *just* brain dysfunction. There is enough coherent meaning here to indicate that this figure represents an organized expression of the living psyche. If he were someone whom you had a personal relationship with at some point in the past, then perhaps it could be argued that he was an apparition arising from your memory or personal unconscious. But he appears here too much as a significant collective figure—an icon of our times—to

reduce him to a mere hallucination. Even if everything
he told you had sounded crazy from the viewpoint of
everyday rationality—which again, it did not—I imagine
on a symbolic level it would still have been loaded with
meaning. But I will tell you at this point that there hasn't
been too much symbolism in your vision either, at least
not in the ordinary sense. The behavior of the people in
your vision—not only yourself—is remarkably lucid. I
am not saying that the Teilhard in it is the real Teilhard
any more than the Karen in it is the real Karen. But in
their own way, they are real."

"I don't get what you mean. Either they're real or
they're not."

"Let me tell you a story. When the renowned Jungian analyst Marie-Louise von Franz first met Jung, she
was an 18-year-old university student. In their discussion, Jung mentioned he had a patient who lived on
the moon. Naturally, she took it that he meant that the
patient behaved 'as if' she lived on the moon. On the
contrary, Jung said, the patient *really* did live on *the moon*.
Von Franz went away wondering whether Jung was crazy,
but when she later realized what he meant, she had an
epiphany that changed her life. What Jung was saying was
that the moon was originally understood as the *luna* or
moon of the soul. *This* was the real moon. The ancients,
when they connected the moon with certain goddesses,
certainly weren't thinking of it as the barren rock with
craters that we moderns think of it as. The physical moon
wasn't a *symbol* for them the way we understand symbols
today. It *was* the moon of the soul. Of course, that began
to change when the Greek philosopher Anaxagoras identified the moon as a spherical object that reflected the

light of the sun, but that doesn't mean the psychic moon disappeared, as Jung's patient illustrated. The psyche has its own terrain, its own planets and worlds. And it also has its own people. You can see them every night in your dreams. They're real. They may not be real the way you and I are real, and they may not have the same kind of consciousness you and I have, but they have a life of their own with unique perspectives. That is why we are often surprised by how independently they behave in our dreams."

"This is a romantic notion of the unconscious, that it has a consciousness of its own with beings in it that also have a consciousness of their own."

"It indeed is Romantic. The Romantics were the immediate forerunners of the modern psychology of the unconscious. They were deeply interested in the condition of man before the development of civilization and rational thought. Their ideas on the nature of the imagination foreshadowed a number of Freud and Jung's own concepts. Now, if you don't mind, I'd like to ask *you* to tell *me* a story. You said in our first session that Brecht's play was questionable. What was questionable about it to you?"

Caught off-guard by Gellert's abrupt change of topic, I had to gather my thoughts. I then explained to him that I believed the play gave the wrong impression about Galileo. Brecht portrayed him as a weakling and coward who, under pressure from the Inquisition, recanted the theory that the sun, rather than the Earth, is at the center of the universe. I said that I could appreciate what Brecht was trying to do. He was writing around the time of the Second World War and was making a social critique against tyrannical authority. He was also, in the aftermath of Hiroshima, arguing that scientists should assume greater social responsibility. But did he have to paint Galileo, whom Einstein rightly called the father of modern science, as an anti-hero because he recanted the heliocentric theory in order to save his skin? This was no more a sign of weakness or cowardice than American or British soldiers publicly confessing their so-called war crimes at the gunpoint of their Iraqi, Iranian, or Afghani captors. We must remember that the philosopher Giordano Bruno was burned at the stake some thirty years earlier for advocating the same sun-centered theory. If anything, Galileo was a hero. He shrewdly objected to two points the Church wanted him to confess to, and these were consequently removed from his official confession. The first was that he was not a good Catholic, and the second that he deceived others in publishing his theory. That was the wink he gave to the camera, so to speak. It was his way of saying to posterity, if not his own audience, that one could believe that the sun is the center of our galaxy and still be a good Catholic, and that in fact there is nothing deceptive about the heliocentric theory.

"I see your point," Gellert said. "But all the same, what is the *story* of Galileo?"

"What do you mean?"

"What is his contribution to humanity, to history?"

"Plenty. In addition to heliocentrism, you could include his work in physics and mathematics, his improvements to the telescope, his astronomical discoveries—I believe he discovered three of Jupiter's four moons. Also his various inventions. Didn't he invent the first thermometer and microscope? The list goes on and on. He was even the first to write about sunspots. What are you getting at, Michael? What does this have to do with anything we're talking about?"

"It has everything to do with what we're talking about. Daniels is the actor or persona of Galileo. He is like an onion. The outer skin is Daniels, but just below is Galileo. His role as Galileo was your first association to him, even before you associated him to your wife. He brings you to Teilhard. In various tales of the hero's journey, this would be analogous to the guide or helper along the way, like the Scarecrow, Tin Man, and Lion aiding Dorothy on her quest to find the Wizard. To begin to appreciate the significance of Teilhard, you may need to start with Daniels, going through his layers. You've already told me Daniels's story—what he means in your psyche. I think there is more there, but for now let's come back to Galileo's story. Would you agree that heliocentrism is his main contribution?"

"Of course," I said.

"But that's not the whole story. He didn't develop the heliocentric theory. He merely proved it with his telescope—no small feat, granted, but it wasn't his idea."

"Of course not. He proved Copernicus was right. It was Copernicus who conceived that the Earth revolves around the sun. The Greeks knew it, too, and the Muslims suspected it, but Copernicus established it as the cornerstone of modern astronomy. So what?"

"We just peeled the second layer off the onion," Gellert said. "Now what's the story of Copernicus?"

"I don't know anything about his life, other than he was born in Poland and educated in Cracow and Italy."

"I'm not asking about his personal life. I'm interested in his significance for humanity."

"Clearly, he introduced the Copernican revolution, one of history's greatest intellectual revolutions. It catapulted the Middle Ages from the thinking of Ptolemy to modern scientific thought. That was the paradigm shift that knocked Christianity's hegemonic view of the universe off its pedestal. After that nobody could argue with any credibility that the Earth and the humanity inhabiting it are the center of the universe."

"Thank you," Gellert said. "That's what I wanted you to put your finger on. Now, let's imagine the same is true in the world of the psyche. Let's imagine that the ego, or consciousness, is the Earth, and as the Earth revolves around this great fiery body, the sun, so too the ego revolves around this other, greater center of the psychic galaxy that casts its own light."

"It sounds Jungian to me."

"That's right. Jung initiated a Copernican revolution in psychology. Freud believed that the ego is the only conscious agent of the psyche and that the material in the unconscious is by and large derived from conscious experience. Jung by contrast saw the ego as orbiting an unconscious source of knowledge that is not derived from consciousness—at least modern man's consciousness—and that, being far greater than the ego, could exert its influence at will. Maybe it's significant that you were guided by the actor of Galileo, and by inference, Copernicus."

"I believe in Occam's razor, Michael. The best explanation for something is usually the one that is simplest.

I want you to help me understand this experience, but I don't want you to rule out a physiological explanation or a Freudian one or any other that will make sense of it in a simple but scientific way."

"Request duly noted," Gellert said.

"Can you provide such an explanation?"

"Sure. How about the one Teilhard himself provided? He indicated that all he wants is for you to think about his ideas and see if they have any relevance. What makes more sense than that, and what could be more simple?"

I did not feel like Dorothy in the land of Oz, but rather like Alice falling down the rabbit hole into Wonderland.

Fourth Installment
The Boldest Interpretation
of the Apocalypse

I am eager to hear Karen's thoughts on our dinner discussion up to now.

"What captivates me about Pierre's philosophy," she says, "is its description of evolution as the drama of God. I know that scientists like yourself say he imbues evolution with divinity, and that the Church called him a heretic who sees evolution as revelation and revelation as a symbol of evolution. But I like the fact that he is an intellectual renegade. My own interest is in a kind of renegade literature—that of the Renaissance, with its revival of old world ideas and yet burgeoning new perspectives on life. Pierre's philosophy sheds much light on a type of Renaissance literature that has always fascinated me—apocalyptic literature. His ideas connect the drama of evolution to the drama of the end of the world as depicted in this literature."

I don't know what I was expecting her answer to be, and given the dinner conversation so far, I suppose I should not be surprised by it, but I am. Or am I surprised

rather by her? She is married to a boor but is an aficio-
nada of the Renaissance.

"How do his ideas connect evolution and the end of
the world?" I say.

"Neither in the traditional religious way nor in the
scientific way you discussed before, with the cosmos dis-
sipating or the sun going nova. Apocalyptic literature,
from the Bible to modern science fiction, approaches the
Apocalypse as a cataclysm. The first apocalypse, brought
on by humanity's arrogance and sinfulness, was Noah's
Deluge in the Old Testament's Book of Genesis. God
promised to never flood the world again, but he did not
promise that there would never be another apocalypse.
Human sinfulness and evil still rampant, the Old Testament Prophets then predicted a second Apocalypse, a
final Day of Judgment."

"Armageddon."

"Yes, the New Testament returns in its concluding
book, the Book of Revelation, to the Old Testament,
referring to the place of the Apocalypse as Armageddon.
The vision of John, the author of the Book of Revelation, is a complex version of how the Prophets saw the
end of the world. John prophesied a drama that will
unfold over a thousand years and involve a fiery bat-
tle with the Antichrist. In the end, the world will be
restored to a paradisaic condition, a 'new heaven and a
new earth.'"

"But I understand that biblical scholars have shown
that this imagery was grafted into the text later, and that
it reflects historical events. Isn't it widely accepted that
the Prophets were predicting the fall of the empires

that occupied Israel and John was predicting the fall of Rome?"

"These historical predictions subtly merge with the prediction of a grand transformation of the world at large at the end of time. The imagery borrows from both inner and outer worlds, and speaks to both inner and outer worlds."

"Have some more wine," Daniels says to me. "It's good for the hardening of your categories."

"No, thank you," I say.

"A possible clue to the actual meaning of the Apocalypse," Karen says, "can be gleaned from the language of the New Testament itself. It describes this event as the 'close of the age.' This didn't necessarily mean the end of the world, but rather, the end of the world *as we know it*. The authors of the New Testament seem to have envisioned this end of their era as occurring in their lifetimes or soon after, just as Jesus himself spoke of his return as if it were imminent. The Church, of course, had to reinterpret the Second Coming as a long-range prospect when this didn't happen. What if the Apocalypse, the coming of the new heaven and earth, is how the New Testament authors intuited the emergence of the noosphere and Omega Point? Naturally, they conceived this in the language and symbolism of their culture and times."

"That is indeed the boldest interpretation of the Apocalypse I ever heard," I say. "Are you telling me that you take seriously this absurd biblical fantasy, here merely given a face lift and repackaged as a utopian scheme of evolution?"

Daniels looks at Karen, but her eyes are riveted on me. I look at Teilhard, whose eyes are glued on me, too.

"Yes," she says. "I take it seriously."

The table becomes silent. Daniels gets up and gets a bottle of Perrier.

"Look," Karen says, "you have to appreciate that the mind is a profound force with its own laws and not just the result of brain neurocircuitry. In the first and very long phase of the mind's development in human history, consciousness struggled to be born. Now it is about to take another huge and lengthy, time-consuming step. This one will be into the realm of the noosphere, a phenomenon of the mind's own mysterious evolution. The first step was traumatic because in its struggle to become conscious, humanity had to learn how things operate—that causes have effects, and effects have causes, and that some of these are good, and others not. This is why in the Book of Genesis consciousness begins when Adam and Eve eat of the Tree of Knowledge of Good and Evil. Moral consciousness above all is not easy to develop. Now the next step of consciousness will be traumatic for the opposite reason: humanity will have to *give up* some of its old notions of how things operate and replace them with new ones that reflect the higher level to which it is evolving. Didn't Einstein say that we cannot solve our problems at the same level of thinking at which they were created? All apocalyptic literature has one thing in common: it demands us to strip away old modes and shift to a new level of thinking. Pierre describes this kind of upheaval as a crisis of reflection. Things no longer make sense, and the world no longer makes sense. War, desperation, all-consuming desire and ambition, disillusionment, the danger of global disaster—these are among the main themes of apocalyptic literature. Your world is in an apocalyptic time defined by these themes."

Having finished eating, I drink some water and collect my thoughts.

"I'm not clear," I say, "whether you are talking about the Apocalypse as the end of evolutionary time, or as the particular apocalyptic time we are now in, this period of human history."

"Both," she says. "*This* particular apocalyptic time marks the beginning of the end of evolutionary time. Although that process of ending, till we reach the Omega Point, will be *very* long, its beginning is announced by humanity's struggle to become conscious of the noosphere. This struggle is itself just in its infancy. Discovering the noosphere involves a gigantic leap up the ladder of consciousness, leaving a whole world and stage of development behind. As Pierre said, this is like a caterpillar breaking out of its skin. Very turbulent. Just look at your world."

I am hard-pressed for a serious response to these vague and ethereal notions. After a moment, Karen says, "I see Pierre's work as a modern form of apocalyptic literature. He is similar to the artist, whom Ezra Pound once described as the antenna of the race. During the

Renaissance, artists like Dante, Milton, and Albrecht Dürer were the antenna of the race—faithful witnesses that some great transformation is coming. More recently, there is Yeats and Eliot, science fiction writers like Arthur C. Clarke, Isaac Asimov, and Philip K. Dick, and other contemporary authors like Doris Lessing, P. D. James, and Cormac McCarthy. And of course, there's good ol' rock 'n' roll."

"Rock 'n' roll?"

"Yes, from Bob Dylan to Bruce Springsteen, U2, and a host of others, many of the great ballads of rock 'n' roll forecast a coming cataclysm and transformation, and often in biblical imagery. Their lyrics are part of the Western tradition of apocalyptic literature no less than the works of the Renaissance."

Teilhard asks me if there is something else I would like to eat or drink. I thank him and say that I am fine.

"Surely," Karen says, "you must have encountered some evidence of an apocalyptic principle of transformation in evolution. In the world of art this principle was nicely summed up by Picasso when he said that every act of creation is first of all an act of destruction."

I explain that the closest thing in evolutionary thinking to what she calls an apocalyptic principle is catastrophism. It holds that the Earth has been shaped not only by slow, incremental processes like erosion, but also by sudden, violent catastrophes such as asteroids and comets impacting it. This theory began with the observation that fossils are the remains of successive generations of flora and fauna that have perished due to such catastrophes. What is interesting is that younger layers of fossils contain more complex species, while older layers are more primitive. One would think that the catastrophes would have diminished the capacity of species to evolve. But it seems that they actually served evolution. They compelled species to adapt in more sophisticated ways.

"Such is the ferocity of biological life," I say. "But that is nature, Karen, a blind force that is indifferent to whether species in fact survive or not, much less suffer. Am I to understand that, because you believe this Apocalypse has an end-point that is desirable, you condone the cataclysm that would bring it about?"

"Of course not. No one wants to see the Earth in flames unless they are a millenarian who takes scripture literally and believes that destroying the world will bring about a heaven on earth or a utopia."

"A senseless loss of life is always tragic," Teilhard adds. "To avoid this humankind must choose to evolve rather than be forced to by a trauma or crisis. It must change and act ethically voluntarily rather than as a last resort. But if a cataclysm is the only way for humanity to evolve, I fear evolution will provide one."

"That's assigning some intended direction to evolution," I say.

"Yes, it is," Teilhard says. "Evolution seeks greater and greater consciousness, even if the numbers of people beholding it decrease."

"But there is no fixed way this must unfold," Karen says. "That would be fatalism. That the Apocalypse or end of our age—of our old order or way of doing things—must happen is part of our fate, but how it happens depends upon us. Someone once wisely said that the best way to predict the future is to create it."

"That is why I have arranged for you to be brought here," Teilhard says to me. "That is what I want you to think about."

"Why me?"

"Because your approach to science lacks religious imagination. To introduce the prospect of the Omega Point into the human condition without violence, great imagination is needed. If a scientist like yourself can imagine the possibilities of evolution, then others could too. And then perhaps this broader vision of the purpose for which human beings were put on the Earth will help them to avoid a cataclysm."

"In my view," I say, "religious imagination is an escape from reality, not a way to better understand it."

"Why do you think that?" Daniels says. "What in science has confirmed to you that religious truth is implausible? I'm not talking about all the religious stories and myths that attempt to explain the various mysteries of life. I'll admit these often have a fantasy quality, as people at that time did not have science as a way to explain things. But what about a simple appreciation for the possibility that beyond the physical universe there may be things that cannot be seen by the naked eye or measured by technical experiments? Or that there may be states of mind that transcend ordinary consciousness?"

"I think that is where religious imagination steps beyond its limits. It's one thing to speculate and express awe, it's another to become dogmatic and authoritarian in one's belief in things which cannot be known with any degree of certainty. In fact, within its limits, I think that religion is a natural and perhaps necessary development of human evolution."

"You do? How so?" Daniels asks.

"Religion initially developed as a way to explain all that was incomprehensible—birth and death, the seasons and fertility cycles, the movements of the sun and moon, floods and droughts, and so on. The fear of death is an especially important factor here. It is a sophisticated emotion that evolved as consciousness and intellect evolved. Animals have an instinctual fear of being preyed upon and harmed, but they do not fear—because they cannot conceptualize—the nonexistence that comes with death. Because humans are more evolved in their thinking they have the capacity to contemplate their mortality, to ask questions like, 'What will happen after I die?' But the dread of death is so overwhelming that religion in turn *had* to evolve as a way to manage it. As humanity evolves out of its childhood and learns to tolerate the fact that the universe is a hostile environment of impersonal forces that reveal no preconceived, intelligent plan or purpose, it will also grow out of its need to believe in a benevolent, superparent being or life after death. Religion will become a facet of our past, like the stone tools early man used to hunt and prepare food. In the meantime, it clearly promotes adaptation by helping people live with their terror of the inevitable. But when it acts as an agent of oppression and war, as has so often been the case, I would say the adaptation has become mal-adaptive."

"*Oui, je sais,* that is the stock explanation of most evolutionary theorists," Teilhard replies. "But this again backs into things by way of how or why they evolved. Even if religion evolved that way does not mean that its metaphysical assertions are invalid. That these are dogmatic and authoritarian merely reflects that religion is itself still at an early and immature stage of its development. It has the same distance to go in order to reach an authentic appreciation of the Omega Point as science. As for religion's history of oppression and aggression, no one can deny that there is truth to that. We all know about the Inquisitions and Crusades. Religion, like any social body, can develop ailments and decay. Yet it is also the oldest body of knowledge in any civilization, and as such is the transmitter of much goodness and wisdom, too. The spiritual teachings and exercises of Saint Ignatius of Loyola, the founder of the Jesuits, are an enduring legacy. With the colleges and universities they established, the Jesuits were prime movers and shakers in the Renaissance. However, the religion of the future must move beyond constrictive social forms that define the individual's personal religious experience. Above all other considerations, Christianity must consist of one's intimate relationship with the cosmic Christ who resides in one's own psyche. The noosphere will evolve not as an organized social form—like a United Nations—but as an organic expression of the interconnected consciousness of many individuals. This process by which humans become more fully human and realize their possibilities, I call hominization, and I see it as central to evolution, including the evolution of both religion and science. Come. Let us go into the living room. We will have some dessert."

Fourth Appointment
Shattering Old Containers
of Meaning

Gellert inquired about my family and any new developments. I explained that not much had changed between my wife and me. Regarding Rachel, Karen and I had gently discussed with her, both separately and together, the behavior problem in question. Our approach was to appeal to her empathy by asking her to imagine how she would feel if she were ignored or pushed out of a social situation. Naturally, as a child she showed limited awareness of her motivations, but she seemed to be beginning to understand how this behavior might affect others.

Gellert then wanted to know my thoughts about Karen vis-à-vis the Karen in my hallucination, or as he called it, vision.

"I never heard her discuss the Apocalypse as such," I said, "though the passionate concern with the future of the world in light of its current problems is similar. Certainly, Karen is a Renaissance scholar."

He asked about her arrangement with the university at which she teaches. I told him she is on leave for another year and then will go back and teach part-time. Motherhood has been her priority.

"Did anything strike you in a particular way in this last installment?" I finally said.

"Yes. To begin with, you wrote that Karen is married to a boor. What do you make of that?"

"Are you insinuating that I'm a boor?"

"Let's put it like this: do you have a boorish shadow you are unaware of, and if so, exactly in what way is it boorish?"

"If I'm unaware of it, how should I know?"

"You're a bright man. Take a look at it right now and raise your awareness." I could see Gellert was in an in-your-face mode again.

"Karen points out now and again how I could be insensitive to others. She feels that when I reach a judgment about them, I could write them off quickly and be indifferent, sometimes even rude."

"Like Rachel?"

"What are you getting at? I'm the reason she's behaving the way she does?"

"Our children sometimes act out our shadows if we haven't integrated them."

I weighed his words carefully, trying not to be defensive. "I suppose I don't suffer fools lightly," I said.

"How does your judgmental quality affect your teaching?" he asked.

"I manage to suspend it with students—how did Bertrand Russell put it? the value of suspended judgment? They're there to learn, I'm there to teach. I don't expect them to be knowledgeable." I was, of course, being partly facetious and partly truthful.

Gellert was staring out the windowed French doors of his office, staring at his Zen rock garden. His forehead was furrowed. "You seem distracted," I said.

"I'm just wondering . . . wondering what it's like to be in your skin."

"Why? Am I so strange to you?"

"No, not strange. But perhaps estranged."

"Estranged from what?"

"From yourself."

"What do you mean?"

"You show little curiosity about yourself. You're interested in figuring out what happened to you during your operation, but you show little interest in exploring your inner workings. You're one of those rare psychologists who never went to a therapist, even if just to check it out once or twice to see what all the fuss is about. In fact, I suspect you're a psychologist who does not even know what the psyche is."

"*What the hell does that mean!?* Everything I teach is about the evolution of human behavior, the patterns of the mind or psyche!"

"Behavioral patterns are a *manifestation* of the psyche. One can be quite knowledgeable about them without having direct knowledge about their living source. It is like seeing light without understanding that it comes from the sun."

"We're back to the sun again, are we?"

"Yes, we are."

"What does that have to do with anything?"

"I imagine it's what your vision is fundamentally about. In its own way, it's an apocalyptic vision."

"How so?"

"It is itself a constellation of the Apocalypse archetype. This is the archetype or instinct of the psyche that comes into play with all apocalyptic events, whether actual or prophesied. As Karen mentioned in your vision, Noah's flood and the coming Apocalypse are two such events, but there are others that are actually historical. The Babylonian exile and Roman occupation—both playing a significant role in the Bible—the Black Death, the Lisbon earthquake, the American Civil War, the two world wars of the last century, were all apocalyptic. To many who suffered their effects, it felt as if the world were ending. Even 9/11 and the so-called war between Islam and the West have raised apocalyptic anxieties. It's no accident that you dreamed of Auschwitz, an apocalyptic event unparalleled in history. However, it's important here to recognize that the Apocalypse archetype does not manifest only collectively. It also constellates in the experience of individuals, primarily as a psychological death and rebirth. Karen mentioned Dante, Eliot, and Dylan. Artists of their kind undergo an apocalypse in their personal lives and then use this experience to inform their art. Of course, ordinary people experience it too, whenever their lives go through a cataclysmic upheaval, be this an illness, a failure of some kind, a divorce, the loss of a loved one, or a midlife crisis. Does any of this resonate with you?"

"I can connect the dots, Michael," I said.

"What is dying and struggling to be reborn in you, Richard?"

"My fundamental understanding of the universe is under attack, not to mention my sense of well-being in it. Nothing unhinges your confidence in your ability to adapt and survive more than brain surgery. One minute you're healthy, the next you are told that they need to open your head to repair a life-threatening aneurysm and there's no sure guarantee how you'll come out of it. Your very mind may not function and be the same. The mere contemplation of this is life-altering, Michael, even if you come out healthy in the end. I had so little time for this to sink in before the surgery, that it is sinking in these recent weeks. I'm realizing that I'm in some kind of post-traumatic shock. And this on top of my separation. I was barely getting adjusted to living alone when I went into the hospital. I'm still not adjusted to it. I miss my children, I miss my wife, I miss my old life. I have no idea what the future holds. Now my child has behavior problems and I am not able to be fully there to deal with them. And, as if all this weren't enough, there's the internal chaos caused by this crazy experience I had under anesthesia. My commitment to scientific investigation obliges me to treat it seriously. Even if it were only a hallucination, I must understand why something so radically opposite to my way of thinking and outside my range of experience has forced itself upon me. Is my own mind trying to tell me something? This experience brings my basic assumptions of not only psychology but evolution itself—assumptions I have built my career on—under scrutiny. Just a moment ago my analyst told me that he thinks I don't even know what the psyche is! Even my religious sensibilities have been assaulted by this experience. *Everything* is in upheaval! What am I to make of all this? I think it's fair to say I'm undergoing an apocalypse."

Gellert remained quiet. I apologized for getting upset.

"There's no need to apologize," he said. "It's important that you inhabit your apocalyptic state fully." He continued to remain quiet.

Finally, I said, "Is this your technique, Michael, to open me up emotionally, get me real vulnerable with my defenses down, and then go after my beliefs?"

"No, I don't look at this process as a war in which it's my job to find your vulnerabilities and shoot your defenses down. And I have no vested interest in going after your beliefs. I'll explore them with you, but I have no investment in changing them. If anything, it seems as if your vision itself is intent on doing that. Speaking of beliefs, can you tell me what religious sensibilities have been assaulted?"

"Michael, let me correct a misunderstanding you may have, one that I think Karen also has. Because I'm not religious in a traditional way does not mean I have no sense of religious appreciation. I am in profound awe of this cosmos we live in, and of the miracle of our existence and evolution into the complex beings we are. I may not ascribe a divine meaning or design to the universe, but I have a deep feeling for its beauty. That is what attracted me to evolutionary science in the first place. The assault I am undergoing seems to be from this thing that you've called the living psyche. Obviously there is something very intelligent inside my mind that is not me as I know myself and that has designed this anesthesia experience. Now that goes against the grain of all my convictions. This intelligence is not something either evolutionary psychology or Bertrand Russell talk about. I am reminded of his famous essay, 'A Free Man's Worship.' There is no higher God, outside us *or* inside us. If it is inside us, *we* are it."

"Isn't that what Teilhard is really saying?"

"It is and it isn't. He may have believed God is nature and inside us, but he still believed in a transcendent Being of some kind."

"For the sake of argument, put the transcendence aside for a moment. It's a thorny problem. Let's stay with the intelligence of the unconscious. How do you imagine this connects to the things Karen was telling you about the Apocalypse?"

"What resonates most with me is her notion of the Apocalypse as the end of an era. I feel that one era of my life has ended and another is, as you would say, struggling to be born. But I don't yet know what that is. Everything is in transition, maybe even my views on the intelligence of the unconscious."

"That's one thing apocalyptic experiences do: they open us up, shattering old containers of meaning so new ones can emerge."

"This Apocalypse archetype, what else can you tell me about it?"

"Its purpose is precisely to reveal this intelligence of the unconscious. As the Jungian analyst Edward Edinger said, the Apocalypse signifies the coming of our essential self into conscious realization. Bringing a perspective beyond the ego's, this self is often at the heart of our dreams, visions, and religious experiences. It is the sun of our psychic galaxy. The Teilhard of your vision, a wise old sage who conveys some special, higher truth, is in fact an image of this. The Apocalypse is a flooding or fiery explosion of the higher self. It comes as a pent-up, compensatory reaction to some extreme attitude that needs to transform. Your personal apocalypse is in this regard curiously related to the Apocalypse the world is facing today. Our world is under the spell of the Apocalypse archetype not only because it is on the brink of catastrophe—almost every generation tends to feel it's on the brink of catastrophe—but also because our belief systems about this higher intelligence are no longer meaningful the way they used to be. The concept of God, at least in our Western traditions, no longer holds up. It is either anachronistic, nonexistent, or fundamentalist. Our religious attitude needs to change. You'd be surprised how much of Jung's thought here coincides with Teilhard's."

"Let me understand. You are saying that traditional images of God are reflections of this unconscious intelligence. So Freud was right: God is a projection."

"If by that you mean he is *no more* than a projection, that's wrong. Remember, the ego is just a small planet orbiting a much greater intelligence in a large psychic solar system. The inner or psychological dimension of this is *real*. The experience of God as being outside of us—as being other than a psychic reality—is itself part of Western man's religious problem today, necessitating an apocalyptic transformation. People can no longer sustain belief in a simplistic, detached God somewhere out there who looks like the God of Michelangelo in the Sistine Chapel. And naturally, only a civilization that sees God as outside of everything could feel it has permission to turn the Earth into a cesspool or garbage can for its waste. An Apocalypse in the outer world would only mirror the eclipse of God in the inner one."

"How does Jung's thought coincide with Teilhard's?" I asked.

"On a number of points. In addition to their ideas of a collective psyche that connects all humanity together at some fundamental level, there is their mutual understanding of the future evolution of consciousness. It is curious that in your vision Teilhard said that a great revolution in consciousness is beginning. Jung felt this way, too. The Apocalypse is essentially this great revolution. Its main characteristic will be the transformation of the Western God-image, by which he meant the Christian concept of God. He agreed with Teilhard that the current image or concept no longer grips people's imaginations. But more importantly, he believed that everything that has been split off from the present Western God-image needs to be reclaimed for a fuller experience not only of the divine, but of humanity itself, since 'man was created in the image of God.' Where, for example, is the instinctual, primitive, animal side of God? We know it exists because the Bible tells us so, and of course, we are speaking here only of the Western, biblical God. The Old Testament's Leviathan and Behemoth, both great beasts of the underworld, represent this side of him. When legend tells us they will be eaten at the Messianic Banquet by the survivors of the Apocalypse, it is implied that this side of the divine will be integrated by humanity."

"That's just an interpretation. It hardly means that God himself was viewed by the biblical authors as an animal."

"Take another biblical image if that one is not convincing. When the Book of Exodus states that God placed

Moses in the cleft of a rock and revealed to him his 'back parts,' what do you think it is really saying?"

"Don't tell me. Not his . . ."

"Yes. Go on."

"His *ass?* God has an ass?"

"According to the Old Testament, yes, just like any primate. He's an animal. In fact, according to Ezekiel's vision, he's three-quarters animal. In the center of God's chariot, Ezekiel saw four creatures, each with four faces, that of a lion, an ox, an eagle, and a human. Jung often referred to this biblical image. He also observed how animals in our dreams can be images of the higher self, or God. To many people this might sound like a harking back to pagan religion. In fact, the pagan side of God must be reintroduced into religion in a modern way in which our animal passions can once again thrive but not, as in early times, rule out the possibility of an ethical consciousness. Both sides are needed. The instinctual is needed in order to restore to God his complete nature, and by extension, do the same to us. Again, only a civilization that sees God and spirit as the opposites of instinct and matter could feel justified in the way it treats the Earth.

For a few quiet moments I had a chance to absorb all that Gellert was telling me. It struck me as curious that the Bible itself inherently supports our animal side, if not our animal origins, and that by extension, it supports the conservation of the Earth.

"And what about the feminine side of God?" Gellert said. "We know that it exists, too. In his Proverbs and Book of Wisdom, Solomon speaks of wisdom as a distinctly female spirit who is an emanation of God. She's the Israelite version of the Greek goddess Sophia, after whom philosophy, or the 'love of wisdom,' was named. What do you imagine the popular fascination with *The Da Vinci Code* was really about? It is true that patriarchal consciousness needed to emerge with all that it has brought—law, ethics, science. But true wisdom, as Solomon knew, involves a feminine receptivity and relatedness to things. This is in dire shortage these days, don't you think?"

"Yes, I sometimes wonder if in certain ways, particularly around our attitudes to the Earth and how we interact with it in comparison to others species, we've devolved rather than evolved. Indigenous peoples like the Native Americans or Australian aborigines seem to have had a balanced, healthier relationship to the Earth. We've advanced scientifically and technologically, but at a great cost to our humanity and to the Earth itself."

"Yes. To evolve, humanity had to sacrifice certain vital parts of itself, which are now screaming to be seen and heard again. Our instinctual, animal side had to be repressed for the ego, superego, and civilization to develop just as the feminine had to be reined in for patriarchal consciousness to emerge, but the cost of both diminishments has been great."

"I understand that our instinctual, animal side—the id—appeared on the scene of evolution before the ego, superego, and civilization. But there's not much historical evidence that matriarchal societies existed before patriarchal ones. Most anthropologists, many of them women, have debunked this idea."

"I know," Gellert said. "I'm not speaking about the organization of societies, but rather the consciousness of cultures. Societies governed by women—what most people mean by 'matriarchy'—are exceptions, but there can be little doubt that ancient cultures worshipped mother goddesses and the Earth Mother before the Father-God. As with nature in general, the mother principle precedes the father one."

"So you are saying the Apocalypse will return us to this?"

"Not exactly return. That would be a regression. To align solely with either one principle or the other involves psychic splitting. Progression, or evolution, requires us to *integrate* them, to hold them together at the same time. This applies not only to the animal and civilized sides of the God-image, and its feminine and masculine sides, but to its good and evil sides. That is perhaps the most subtle yet profound dissociation of all—the dark, evil side of God."

"Assuming for a moment that there is a God, how could such a side of him exist? He would hardly be a god worth having if he were dark and evil?"

"I'm talking again about the Western, biblical image of God. We know this side of him exists because the Bible explicitly tells us so. What does God say to Isaiah? 'I form the light, and create darkness: I make peace, and create evil: I the Lord do all these things.' Christianity, as Jung argued, has split this off from God and put it all on the devil."

"What's the difference," I asked, "whether the principle of evil is put on God or the devil? It still amounts to the same thing, that evil has a supernatural origin."

"It makes a very real difference. The power of ideas is stronger than even armies. It's different when the devil, the evil one, carries the dark principle, and when God himself, the supposedly good one, carries it. It is *too easy* to split evil off, and if we permit it with God, or our idea of God, then we will surely permit it with ourselves. Isn't that what we do with evil? We split it off and project it onto the other. Always the other one is evil, but not we ourselves. Until we can accept that even God has a dark side, we will not be able to accept our own, and there will be one genocide after another."

"But I still don't understand how an omnipotent and omniscient God, if he even exists, could have an evil side."

"Evil exists, doesn't it? We see it everywhere around us, and if we look closely enough, within ourselves, too. It must come from somewhere. The Eastern traditions see it as part of the structure of the universe, as what happens when the original Void enters dualistic form. Teilhard here differed from Jung and in some ways was closer to the East. He saw evil as the principle of imperfection operating in man as a result of his being in the process of becoming. It is the human experience of an impersonal facet of the process of evolution. Jung on the other hand saw evil as a mysterious but distinct psychic force originating in God. Perhaps his most controversial idea was that God is unconscious of his dark side, as he demonstrated by his capricious behavior with Job. There the devil clearly served at God's pleasure. Even in his omnipotence God evidently did not see how he acted this side of himself out through the devil. This speaks again to his back parts. No one can see their own backside, their shadow, without effort. Others can see it more easily and clearly than they do. This appears to have been the case with Job and God. The upside of this, Jung believed, is that man, by wrestling with the evil in his own heart and in the world, helps God become more conscious of the dark side of himself. Not only does God redeem man, but man redeems God."

"What Jung said about God becoming conscious of himself through man sounds similar to what Teilhard said about the noosphere becoming conscious and advancing the evolution of God himself. It's a good thing for Jung he wasn't a priest like Teilhard. He would surely have been censored."

"He had his own difficulties finding acceptance for his ideas. The two thinkers had much in common."

Gellert went on to explain yet another way Jung and Teilhard complemented each other. Jung conjectured three phases in the evolution of Western consciousness based on the three aspects of God in the New Testament. The age of God the Father was the era of the Old Testament. The age of the Son is our current Christian era, now coming to an end—hence the Apocalypse. The next age will be that of the Holy Spirit, an era which Jung envisioned as a celebration of the spirit or psyche and which Teilhard might have seen as the maturation of the noosphere. Instead of seeking God out there somewhere, humanity will discover him within. The new God-image may very likely be the psyche itself, or the intelligent self at its center. The new religious attitude will thus reflect a shift from worshipping an external God to self-realization, focusing on individuation or inner development—the most refined aspect of what Teilhard called hominization. As such, it will incorporate the split-off sides of God *within us* while advancing a genuine ethical awareness.

"If this sounds like pie in the sky," Gellert said, "it should be emphasized that we're not talking about an imminent event. Jung estimated that it will take about six hundred years for this new order of civilization to evolve. It will probably involve great global turmoil, if not also a modern version of the Dark Ages with a return to ignorance and barbarism. We are seeing the beginning of this turmoil already today. In fact, the Apocalypse is not something that *will* happen *one day.* It is already happening."

But pie in the sky was exactly what all this sounded like to me. I wondered to what end these meetings with Gellert were leading.

Second Interlude
Watching Your Child Suffer

It never ceases to amaze me that no matter how clearly I understand the impersonal nature of evolution, the alarm bell that goes off in my mind and heart when my child is endangered is extremely personal. My instincts are so honed to my children's particular cries, that if I'm in a large supermarket and hear a child wailing a few aisles over, I can instantly identify if it is my child or not. Evolution endows us with strong personal bonds in order to assure its impersonal agenda.

Karen's phone call came around 8:00 at night. For the third time in a row, Ben's stool had blood in it, and this time, a significant amount. The next day we had an emergency appointment with Dr. Doreen Howard, a pediatric gastroenterologist. She scheduled a colonoscopy for Ben to take place two days later. He received prep and pep talks from both parents, with promises that he would get three gifts he wanted, depending of course on how well he cooperated. Ben may possibly grow up to be a businessman. Seeing that he had a good hand here, and egged on by his sister, he negotiated with us to include a dog as one of the three gifts—something we had long resisted.

The day before the colonoscopy, Ben underwent a liquid diet and then a fast without any complaint or bad mood. He went into the procedure room and under anesthesia with a brave attitude. When he awoke, he was delirious from the anesthesia, angry, and unhappy. After a spell of crying, he calmed down. But he hated the intravenous drip he needed for the second day without food.

After the procedure the doctor gave us good news with one reservation. The only finding was a single, solitary juvenile polyp in Ben's sigmoid colon. This was the best we could have hoped for. The reservation was that, for a child, it was huge—the size of a walnut, the largest Dr. Howard had ever seen in a child. It was removed successfully, but because of the resulting large surgical wound on the interior sigmoid wall, she was concerned about hemorrhaging which could lead to a life-threatening surgical emergency. Thus Ben was kept for two nights in the hospital. He did well, and there was no evidence of internal bleeding or fever and infection. We had to wait seven days for the final good news that came from the pathology lab: the polyp was benign. It was probably congenital.

As anyone who has had a sick child knows, it is extremely difficult to come to terms with the fact that there's only so much you can do, and that ultimately, it's out of your hands. Nothing is more painful than watching your child suffer. It can be devouring.

I cancelled two appointments with Gellert. He understood.

Fifth Installment
Levels of Evolution?

Dessert is crème brûlée. Karen says she picked it up at a fine pastry shop. It is as delicious as the rest of the dinner. We are all in the living room. Daniels asks if any of us would like coffee, and goes into the kitchen to brew some. Teilhard and Karen get into an animated discussion, but I feel exhausted and can't follow it.

"Are you tired?" Teilhard asks me.

"Yes, very." Given the climb up the mountain in the hot sun, the aperitif, the dinner with wine, this dessert, and whatever other effects I am undergoing in surgery, I'm not surprised.

"You'll be going back soon," Teilhard says. "The worst of your surgery is over."

"How do you know that?"

"It passed as you were speaking with Karen."

When Daniels returns he wryly announces that he didn't make any coffee for me. "Why waste this fine roast from the Nilgiri Mountains of South India on someone who thinks it's a hallucination?"

"Marc, you are joking," Karen says. He serves each of us a cup, myself included. We sit quietly for a while, enjoying the crème brûlée and coffee.

"Nothing like a good café to wake you up," Daniels says, winking at me. "Tell me, Professor Darwin, if you really think all this is a hallucination, why didn't you simply tell us all to get lost as soon as you reached that conclusion?"

"A hallucination can mimic and induce conditions in the real world. I'm not sure what might happen to me on the operating table if I were to tell you to get lost. Perhaps you are personifications of a neuroprotective mechanism that I need for my survival."

"You have a scientific answer for everything, don't you?"

"How am I going to get back?" I ask Teilhard. "Do I need to go back down the mountain?"

"No, it's much easier the other way," Daniels answers.

"Your body is already at the location that your subtle body needs to return to," Teilhard says.

We sit silently again.

Feeling invigorated from the coffee, I say, "This parallel universe, how parallel is it? Are there wars here, and danger of ecological collapse?"

"There are social groups," Teilhard says. "Civilization, and the *quest* for civilization, are similar. This particular world is one among many in the plane immediately above yours. It is, so to speak, a blueprint of your world, a kind of binary opposite and complement, crystallizing both the enduring essence and the future of your world. It is an extension of your world but uninhibited by the restraints and causality of time and space. So no, there are no wars here or danger of ecological collapse because there is no impetus for them. There is nothing to conquer or hold on to."

"How many worlds are there?"

"Thousands and thousands," Teilhard says. "All inhabited. You could think of them, too, as neurons in a vast, interconnected brain or mind."

"And I take it there are thousands of planes, too?"

"*Au contraire.* There are only four planes. They reflect different levels of evolution."

"*Levels* of evolution?"

"Yes. Creation in its entirety is evolving. All of creation is moving toward the Omega Point—not just the physical dimension—and it is moving all *together*. You come from the fourth and lowest plane, the physical universe. The two planes above become progressively more subtle until they reach the highest plane of pure form or consciousness. The three lower planes are thoughtforms or emanations of this. In the physical plane this source of pure consciousness is obscured. But because the first plane is also the essence of all the others, it is possible to perceive it even in the physical plane. That is what is called a mystical experience. Evolution's ultimate aim is for consciousness—for humanity—to realize its essential mystical condition but with the fullness of what it has gained from its own evolution."

If Teilhard's published ideas are purely speculative, these are altogether esoteric.

"And these planes are what has traditionally been thought of as the afterlife?"

"Yes, among other things as well."

"And you are saying this afterlife is subject to the principles of evolution?" I ask, wondering about the fanciful capacity of my imagination.

"Yes and no," Teilhard says. "On the whole, creation

is evolving—at all levels except the first. But certain principles of evolution that apply on the physical level do not apply on the subtle levels, and vice versa. Because the heavenly spheres have a timeless quality, change happens very slowly here. Heaven is not the static, idle paradise people often think it is. It is a condition of changelessness in change, if you can imagine such a thing. The changelessness makes the change very slow and even lethargic compared to the physical world. The physical dimension, with all its limitations, provides excellent conditions for transformation."

"This is why," Daniels says, "Buddhists believe that a human incarnation is a rare and special privilege. The material world is the most ideal for working out karma."

I feel a tingling sensation come over me. Can it be the coffee?

"Why does the physical dimension provide excellent conditions for transformation if it is so limited?" I ask.

"The rapid passage of time," Teilhard says, "provides combustion for change. There's a pressure that doesn't exist in the heavens. There are things that are very difficult to learn in the heavens because people are not faced with their mortality. Aging, corruption of the body, and death are vital teaching aids. Furthermore, things are experienced with the full force of all that corporeal existence brings—sensuality, passion, longing, lust, pain, suffering, ecstasy, even mystery that veils things so they have a newness and unpredictablity that they don't quite have in the heavens. Evolution here occurs at a much slower pace."

"So is it more advanced or isn't it?"

"It is not a question of more or less. It's not black or white. We are speaking of a single cosmic whole that is evolving at different levels that are not isolated from each other. There is an intricate web of interrelationships between the four planes. From the viewpoint of human evolution the physical plane is the *foundation* of the others. The Earth plays a vital role in the cosmic scheme of evolution. Much can potentially happen in the span of a single lifetime on Earth. The water that goes into the earthly roots of the tree of cosmic evolution nourishes the tree to its very tips. What happens on Earth—or as the case may be, does *not* happen—influences what goes on in the heavens."

"Can you imagine," Karen says, "how many of the millions of young people, the millions of Anne Franks, who lost their lives just in the Second World War alone might have gone on to do great things in the arts, sciences, medicine, and politics? What of *all* the millions who lost their lives in other wars, holocausts, natural disasters, and epidemics due to nature or human ignorance? Lost opportunities for the development of consciousness on Earth have to be made up somewhere, and that is not so easy on the heavenly side. That is why it is important for us here what happens now ecologically and otherwise in the physical world. If there is a cataclysmic Apocalypse there it will have ramifications here."

The tingling sensation intensifies. My skin is crawling.

"I want to tell you a parable before you leave," Teilhard says. "It's about the key to understanding evolution. There was a man who came home one night and saw his neighbor looking for something under the lamppost in his front lawn. He asked him what he was looking for, and the neighbor said, his key. He asked him if he needed any help, and the neighbor gratefully accepted. So the two searched the front lawn for the key. After a half hour the man said, 'We've looked everywhere. Where exactly did you lose it?' The neighbor said, 'In the backyard.' 'Why then are we looking for it here!?' the man exclaimed. 'Because,' the neighbor said, 'this is where the light is.'"

I feel a rush of blood to my head, as if I'm going to faint. I lean back into the sofa and rest my head on it. I see Teilhard, Daniels, and Karen watching me. Teilhard says, "Relax, it is alright." Karen puts her fingers to her lips and blows me a kiss.

I open my eyes and struggle to get oriented. I am lying in a bed, my back slightly elevated. My first sight is Karen smiling. She takes hold of my hand. My other hand has an IV attached and there's a wire clipped to one of my fingers. There's something in my throat. It feels like someone is pressing their thumb down on it.

A nurse appears and then a doctor. I try to talk but can't. I indicate that my throat is uncomfortable. The doctor tells me I'm intubated and on a ventilator but now that my brain and body have "come back on line" and I'm breathing on my own he's going to remove the tube in my throat. He carefully does so. I realize there are machines all around and that I'm in the ICU. I don't understand any of this, as I think the surgery has not happened yet.

Karen asks me how I feel. Okay, I say in a hoarse voice. The doctor asks me to wiggle my toes, then my fingers. He is checking for coordination and brain damage, but I don't understand this either.

When will the operation be?, I ask. Karen says it's over. It happened two days ago. I've been in a pentobarbital coma since then, she explains. I say that can't be. I have no pain. How could it be after the operation if I have no pain? In spite of the fact that the brain itself has no nerve endings or pain receptors, I am anticipating, if not the kind of headache I had before, at least discomfort from the cutting and drilling of the surgery. The scalp, the meninges that cover the brain, and the periosteum that covers the bone *do* have pain receptors. Karen takes a mirror from my travel bag and places it before me. My head is bandaged. My face is unshaven.

At first I have no recollection of my anesthesia experience. Then, all in a flash, it comes back to me.

Two days later, after having been moved to a private room, Karen brings the children for a visit. I am overjoyed to see them. They are visibly upset by my bandaged head, even though Karen prepared them as best she could. They have presents for me. I unwrap the first box. It is a matching gray sweatshirt and sweatpants. The second box contains a pair of running shoes—Nikes, size nine and a half.

"I know you wear Adidas," Karen says, "but the store was out of your size and the kids insisted."

Fifth Appointment
A Renaissance Soul

Gellert was very interested in Ben. I explained how his ordeal felt as if my own intestines had been cut to pieces.

"I hope you're not going to suggest that Ben's polyp was also an expression of my unintegrated shadow," I said.

"Of course not. But it is an interesting convergence of events, don't you think? Your surgery, Ben's surgery. Your problem digesting what has happened to you, Ben's problem in his digestive system. Troubles in your marriage, troubles with both kids. Apocalypse within, apocalypse in your family. Nikes in the vision, Nikes after the vision."

"You think all this is what Jung called synchronicity, don't you?"

"Don't *you*?"

"No, I think they're coincidences."

"That's what synchronicity is."

"Yes, but doesn't Jung say it has a purpose behind it, that it's not an accident or random occurrence?"

"That's right. Synchronicity is a meaningful coincidence. If it has no underlying meaning or connection, the coincidence is simply synchronous, but not synchronistic. Don't you think there might be some meaning to these coincidences?"

"No. When it rains, it pours, that's all. As for the two pairs of Nikes, that was pure chance. Things like that happen."

"Okay."

I looked at Gellert, wondering what to talk about first. I decided to begin with the brain's mental representation of what was happening to it. "After the surgery," I said, "I learned that the aneurysm burst in the late afternoon. Teilhard indicated that this happened at the time I was talking with Karen. That was also late afternoon. In other words, the experience seemed to be happening in real time. It's as if the Apocalypse that we were discussing *was* the emergency of my aneurysm bursting."

"What does that mean to you?"

"It suggests that the brain was monitoring the entire event, perhaps the way it marks time with its circadian clock." Circadian rhythms are the sleep cycles of the brain, cued by light and darkness. Jet lag, for example, is a disruption of these rhythms.

"Okay."

I wondered why Gellert had so little to say about this. "There's another conclusion I've reached connected to timing," I said. "If this was happening in real time, and I was 'returned' into my body as the surgery was ending, as Teilhard implied, then this altered state had to be related to the anesthesia. The anesthesia was wearing off by then because the pentobarbital coma was induced."

"Okay."

"That's all you have to say about this?"

"What else would you like me to say? These are plausible conclusions."

"They don't compel you to conclude that this was really an anesthesia phenomenon?"

"Yes, it was very likely an anesthesia phenomenon. Does that mean it was *only* an anesthesia phenomenon? The living psyche manifests through such phenomena, too."

"Do you think it could have happened without the anesthesia?"

"Probably not. The anesthesia triggered an altered state of consciousness. Your vision reflects this altered state. It doesn't reflect anything about the anesthesia. Untold numbers of people undergo anesthesia. Few if any have experiences like this. Your visionary state resembles the experiences of shamans who take certain hallucinogens to induce such an altered state. That state is as real or valid as this one, merely apprehended with the aid of mind-enhancing substances. As Teilhard said, you happened to be passing by his neighborhood. The neighborhood is there. The anesthesia made it possible for you to visit."

"Well, I could tell you that if I ever need surgery again I'll be very wary about what might happen."

"Why? You make it sound like a bad LSD trip instead of a fine French dinner and a stimulating conversation with one of the most interesting figures of the twentieth century, not to mention your wife."

"That was a crazy experience, Michael. Have you ever had anything like this happen to you?" That was a question I had wanted to ask him since our initial consultation.

"What would it mean to you if I had?"

I could have anticipated he would throw it back to me. "After what I've been through, I wouldn't think you're crazy," I said.

"Even though such experiences defy science and cannot be understood by the scientific method?" he said.

"You think that the very purpose of this experience is to disillusion me of the limits of science, don't you?"

"Not disillusion you—the value of science and the scientific method is no illusion. Rather, unfetter you. Science and the scientific method do not grasp all of reality. Again, I think Teilhard said it succinctly. He wanted to expand your thinking on evolution."

"His ideas are very strange, Michael. What do you think of this notion of four planes of evolution?"

"It's an archetypal idea. The Kabbalists talk of four planes, as do the Hindu mystics. Certain schools of Buddhism also believe that there are four planes of existence. These models aren't entirely identical to each other, yet some of them overlap. Jung saw the number four itself as a symbol of wholeness."

"The fact that the idea is archetypal doesn't prove its veracity, but only explains how it got into my psyche, correct?"

"Yes, that's correct. Archetypes are evolutionary imprints in the psyche. Their powerful force and constant repetition in the course of history have embedded them indelibly in the collective unconscious. Freud referred to them as archaic vestiges. However, you have to wonder why the psyche finds such ideas so powerful and worthy of repetition in the first place—is it only because they relieve our fear of the unknown?—or why mystics like the Kabbalists and yogis, who had no historical influence upon each other, came upon such similar notions."

"What about this other notion of the heavens evolving and the Earth being a kind of rapid-combustion chamber, if I understood Teilhard correctly?"

"It's provocative, don't you think?"

"It reminds me of something Noel Coward said. He said we have no reliable guarantee that the afterlife will be any less exasperating than this one."

"Yes, Jung said something similar that speaks particularly to the significance of this life. Based on his own encounters with the deceased, he thought that the knowledge attained by them in the afterlife does not necessarily surpass what they knew at the moment of death. Hence their interest in the living and their visits to the living in the form of dreams and apparitions. He had the feeling that the dead are standing directly behind us, waiting to hear what answers we will provide for the great questions of human destiny."

"So you believe in the afterlife?"

"I believe that there are mysteries that the conscious, rational mind has not yet fathomed and in and of itself may never fathom."

"Maybe this is what Teilhard meant with his parable about the man and his neighbor looking for the key under the light," I said. "It is logical to look for it under the light of rationality, but that may not unearth the key that will explain the greater mysteries of life."

"That's a good interpretation."

"It might make matters easier if I could believe it, but I cannot. I acknowledge that there are things we don't understand, but that we *can't* understand them is merely a reflection of our current, limited knowledge. Reason is the only way we ever had and will have to truly understand anything. The superstitious belief systems that insist that there exists a heaven after we die and a higher being residing there may have soothed humanity's fear of death, but they also kept it in ignorance for millennia. I accept that there is possibly some meaning or design to this experience that happened to me, but that there are levels of existence or objective psychic realities other than the one we are in right now—the Copernican thing you talked about—I just can't buy it, Michael."

"That's alright. It's not for sale."

With that, we reached an impasse, both anchored in our separate positions.

After some moments, I said, "I'd like to talk about Karen."

"Good," he said.

"I feel we've become closer since my surgery, and now this scare with Ben had the same effect. We always close ranks in a crisis."

"What does 'closer' mean to you?"

"We work as a team. We suffer together and feel joy together. When we were in the doctor's office discussing Ben's options, I could read her thoughts just by looking at her face. I'm sure it's mutual. She feels like family, that's the best way I could describe it."

"I understand."

"I still don't really understand what caused this rift between us that led to our separation, and what would heal it. I'm not saying it's all because of the religious interests she developed, but that seems to have become a kind of signpost for our differences. That's what religion always historically does, isn't it? It divides people against each other even though it preaches love and humanity's oneness in the eyes of God."

"What have you learned from your vision that might help you with regard to this rift?"

"I've been thinking about that. It occurred to me that, quoting Teilhard himself, his world is the essence of our world. If it is a Platonic realm, as he said, then it represents things in their essential forms. I don't know how much this Teilhard was like the real Teilhard, or how accurately his ideas were portrayed, but he seemed like the quintessential Teilhard. What if the Karen in his world was also the quintessential Karen? She didn't get into Renaissance studies because of an overtly religious interest, but maybe that was somehow always 'in there,' an essential motivating factor that only surfaced in recent years. Maybe in some way that was the real Karen, and I never saw it."

Gellert was staring at me as if he were in disbelief. "What's the matter, Michael? You don't think I'm capable of deep thought?"

He laughed. "What surprises me is the *symbolic* thought," he said. "I don't know what the key to understanding evolution is, but the key to understanding dreams and visions is symbolic thinking. The unconscious generally speaks in symbolic images, not ideas. The Karen of your vision is an image whose underlying meaning you are perhaps quite right in describing as a quintessence. In alchemy, the soul was considered to be the fifth element, or *quint-essence*. What then do you think your vision can teach you about Karen's quintessence or soul?"

"I never thought of this before, but it just came to me. I've always admired Karen as a Renaissance scholar and teacher. But I never really clearly saw that she's also a Renaissance soul. I don't believe in the soul, of course, but I mean it in the sense that we speak of someone as a 'good soul.' Karen is truly a *Renaissance soul*. She loves it, she breathes it, she exudes it."

"Can you give me an image of it? It doesn't have to be visual. Even ideas can be looked at as images in the sense that they present a picture."

"Music. The choral music of the Renaissance. I could hear in my head Karen's favorite compositions by Palestrina, so often floating through the rooms of our house. That *Missa Brevis* really is her soul. I never realized that till this moment."

We sat quietly for some time.

"I'm just thinking about her," I eventually said. "You know, it was strange in that dining room. I found her intelligence and spontaneity, her spunk, very appealing. I felt that way when I was courting her. We were young, just students then. There was something very down-home and Midwestern about her, and at the same time, erotically alluring."

Gellert kept his eyes fixed on me, as if waiting for me to say more.

"I miss her, Michael. I feel immense love for her, but I also feel remorse as I recognize that I don't really know her. I don't really appreciate her for who she is, and how sensitive she is—how deeply she feels things, whether issues with the kids or the environment or what's going on politically in our country and the world. Even her criticisms of me are sensitive in that they're well thought-out and delivered in a loving way. I can see how I've taken her for granted, a complaint she has made more than a few times. I wonder how real our years together have been."

"It's very important, all that you've just said. This might be the beginning of your marriage, not the end."

I was carried away by a wave of nostalgia, fleeting memories that make up a life together.

"She married *you*," Gellert said, gently breaking my reverie.

"What?"

"Karen married you, Richard, not Daniels."

A sharp pain shot through my chest. I broke into tears. I don't know whom I wept for—myself, Karen, *us?* I had not cried since I was a child. It felt good, yet I was ashamed. I apologized for my indulgence.

"Have a little self-compassion," Gellert said.

We again sat quietly for some time. I felt tired—exhausted. When Gellert asked me about this, I explained how burdened I had felt these past months. More quiet. Finally, I said, "I wonder if I should tell Karen about my experience during the surgery."

"Why haven't you told her?"

"I wasn't sure how she'd react. I knew she wouldn't think I was crazy. On the contrary, I imagined she'd have great empathy. But I didn't know where she would take it. Would she think it was a divine revelation? Would she take it literally? I needed to arrive at some understanding of it myself before I shared it with her."

"So it had nothing to do with being separated from her? If you were living with her, you still wouldn't have told her?"

"I don't think I would have. I'm less inclined to tell her being separated, as I wouldn't want it to influence her to see me in a different light, especially if I finally concluded the whole thing was nonsense. That would only disappoint her. But I think that even if we were still living together I would have wanted to digest this more fully before coming out with it, even to Karen."

"I see. Where do you feel you are in that process now?"

"I think you've helped me to see that there is at least some personal meaning to this vision, as you call it, and some ways to look at it other than a literal interpretation on the one hand and outright dismissal of it as nonsense on the other. I'm still in the fog about the significance of Teilhard, frankly, and Daniels too, but our discussions about Karen have been illuminating, in a dark sort of way. Curiously, what I relate to most in the vision is this inner Karen's contribution, the Apocalypse. I agree that the world is on the cusp of some dramatic transformation. I don't see this religiously or spiritually, but rather in terms of the ecological hazards we are at risk of and the massive social disruptions these would create."

"What about your own depression, or malaise, as you've called it? How are you dealing with that?"

"You're helping me to see the personal dimension of all this as an apocalypse of a kind, too. That puts everything I've gone through, and am still going through with these recent problems with my kids, into a context. I can at least better understand the malaise and listlessness now. So what do you think? Should I give Karen a copy of these installments I've written for you? I think I have enough clarity to be comfortable doing that, and I think she should know."

"It sounds like you answered your own question. Why are you asking me?"

"I suppose I'm ambivalent. I'm afraid what it will let out of the box."

"What will it let out of the box?"

"I don't know."

"Good. It's good to not always know what will come out of the box."

"I'd like to continue seeing you. I don't think our work is done."

"Fine."

Gellert reached for a brown paper bag on his desk. "I have something for you," he said. He took a bottle out from the bag. It was green and flask-shaped, and above the gold cross on the red label it said, "Unicum." It was identical to the bottle in my vision.

"Where did you get that?" I said.

"From a liquor shop known for its imports. Are you allowed to drink?"

"Lightly."

"Good. We'll have just a sip or two. I don't want you driving home under the influence." Gellert pulled out two schnapps glasses from the same paper bag. He opened the bottle and poured us each a drink. "To your health and recovery, physically *and* psychologically," he said.

After we had a chance to savor our sips, he nodded at my glass and asked, "So what's your assessment?"

"It tastes exactly as it did in my experience."

"And you never had it before?"

"I assume I must have had it somewhere and forgotten about it. Cryptomnesia—hidden memory. How else could it turn up in my vision? What are you trying to prove, Michael?"

"Nothing. Just trying to soften some of the categories." I laughed. "Take it home with you," he said.

Sixth Appointment
The Famous Shadow

I phoned Gellert the day before our next meeting. I told him that I had given Karen the installments, and after reading them she asked if she could come with me to see him. He asked why. I said I didn't know. All she said was that she thought it would be good to have an impartial, third party present. He said he wasn't impartial. He was my therapist and his commitment was to me. She needed to understand that. I said I'd convey that to her. More important, he said, were my own feelings about her coming. I said I'd like her to come. It might be helpful.

Karen and I came together. After Gellert greeted her in the same friendly way he did when he first met me, we all sat down, Karen and I beside each other on the couch. There was some discussion about the children as well as my operation. He also asked her about her professional plans. I think he wanted to give her some footing, a sense of comfort.

Finally he asked her what prompted her to come to this appointment.

"I read Richard's account of his experience," she said, "and frankly, I'm at a loss for words. It is unlike anything of his that I've read—a complete departure from the man I know. It's like Paul on the road to Damascus. But what really upset me was that he didn't feel he could come to me with this. It's not that I resent that he told you before me, but that he felt he had to sort it out before sharing it with me. It's that he couldn't trust exposing himself to me and being vulnerable and confused. He carried this around for weeks bottled up. Anyone could see he was depressed, but no one had a clue what he had been struggling with in his solitude. I'm hurt that he didn't feel he had a partner in me."

"Have you told him this?" Gellert said.

"No, I thought I'd wait till we came here. I feel this reflects a deeper issue in our marriage that we've been going around in circles with, and I finally thought it would be good to meet with a professional."

"Maybe you should tell him," he said.

"I'm telling you, Richard, this hurts. Didn't you feel you had a partner in me?"

"Of course I did, Karen," I said. "But I felt I had to get a handle on this before sharing it with you. I wasn't sure how well you'd tolerate my skepticism and I didn't want to use this to influence your decision about our future. I'm sorry you feel hurt."

"I've tolerated your skepticism well for years. Why did you think that would change?"

"We're not together anymore, Karen."

"And you think that's because of your skepticism?"

"In part."

"What's the other part?"

"One thing I've recognized coming here is that you've been right about my not appreciating you and taking an active interest in things that are important to you. You've complained about that for a while, and I'm beginning to understand that now."

"You keep focusing on our different interests. I don't have a problem with these any more than I do with your skepticism. I think these become a problem as a result of the issue underneath them. When you get so absorbed in your own interests, in your own world, there's no room for me. I don't feel you really relate to me. We've become like two strangers living under the same roof. If we were connected emotionally I wouldn't care about any other differences. I feel I'm alone in this relationship. The fact that you kept me clued out all these weeks from what was going on inside you just proves how separate we are. When I asked for a separation I was only giving voice to the emotional separation already between us."

Although I had heard this before, I was hearing it differently now. It was difficult to hear.

After a moment, Gellert said, "Richard, how do you understand what Karen is saying?"

"I could see how over the years I've become less engaged emotionally with her. Having kids takes so much time and energy—emotional energy, not just physical—that I often feel I have so little left for myself. At the end of the evening when the kids are finally in bed I just want to read and do some writing. It's true that I haven't been very available to Karen."

"That is really just an excuse," Karen said. "You obviously have enough energy to work on something you like. Unfortunately, that something isn't our relationship. But this has nothing to do with the kids. You were like this already well before the kids were born."

"How did that manifest?" Gellert asked Karen.

"After the first year or so of marriage," Karen said, "he gradually stopped being interested. As he got more absorbed in his career, we talked less about intimate things. When the kids came such discussions became even more rare because so much revolves around them. He is a very good father, but as a husband he became emotionally distant and uninterested. If I tried to engage him he'd respond, but with a minimum of personal investment. That's merely the absenteeism. More offensive was how he'd dismiss me. When we'd go over to friends or out for dinner with them he'd show interest in any topic or discussion involving his academic interests. But when it turned to my work or interests he'd become aloof, on a couple of occasions even changing topics midstream. There was a pervasive sense that he and his interests were simply more important. But in truth, this was there from the beginning. I found the fact that Marc Daniels was in his experience very amusing. What did you think of that, Richard?"

"I'm not sure I know what you're referring to," I said.

"You don't remember what happened at his cast party?"

"No."

"You were positively obnoxious."

A vague memory came back to me. I tried to retrieve it more fully.

"What happened, Richard?" Gellert asked.

"As I recall now, just after the toast, as we were drinking champagne, Daniels came over to Karen and me. He asked me what I thought of the play. I told him I thought it was a fine production. He then asked me if I liked his performance—"

"That's not what he asked you," Karen interrupted. "It was over ten years ago, maybe you don't remember. He asked you if you found his Galileo believable."

"Okay, he asked me if I found his Galileo believable. What's the difference?"

"Liking his performance is different than believing it. You can believe something and still not like it. You make it sound like he was fishing for compliments. He was a student just trying to hone his craft."

"Alright, I can accept that. In any event, we got into a discussion on whether it is *believable* that Galileo was a cowardly anti-hero—"

"Again," Karen snapped, "*you* got into that discussion. All he wanted to know was if you found his portrait of *Brecht's* Galileo convincing."

"Well, I just couldn't find anything convincing about it. If the playwright's character portrait is unbelievable, I don't see how the performance can be convincing."

"That's not even the point. He was celebrating his final performance of a four-week run. Why did you even go there with him? You got into a long argument with him and never even answered the question he asked. You were offensive to him and embarrassing to me. And then after, when we went home, I tried to talk with you about it but you got into an argument with me. That's what I mean when I say you're often self-absorbed and inconsiderate."

A long silence followed.

Finally, I said, looking at Gellert, "I guess *there's* the *famous* shadow."

More silence.

"Thank you, Richard," Karen said.

"For what?"

"For not being defensive. For listening."

"Karen, I can work on these things," I said.

"I'm glad to hear that," she said. "It's heartening. Up to now you couldn't even acknowledge them."

"Karen," Gellert said, "what was your reaction to the fact that in Richard's vision you and Daniels were married, and happily, no less?"

"I found that curious. I liked Marc. He seemed like a man in touch with his feelings, and comfortable expressing them. He did make fun of things, including himself. I imagine that Richard's vision was perhaps pointing to a side of himself that he's out-of-touch with, and maybe to a different kind of marriage that *we* could possibly have. Isn't it true, Michael, that in dreams—and I suppose visions too—people represent dissociated parts of ourselves?"

Gellert confirmed that this is often so, especially if we haven't seen these people for a long time or if they're anonymous figures. He added that the relationship in the vision may very likely be compensating for what is lacking in the real one, showing what a more connected, harmonious way of relating looks like.

"I was wondering," I said to Karen, "if you've been having an affair, if that was a factor in your asking me to move out."

"What if I have?"

"I'd be very hurt, Karen."

"*Really?* Sometimes I wonder."

"Why? You don't think I have feelings for you?"

"Sometimes I wonder. As I've told you on a number of occasions, I wonder if you even see me for who I am. I know you love me as your wife and as the mother of your children, but I often have a sense that you don't really know me that well. You don't take the time to find out what's moving inside me, how I'm feeling or thinking about things. You take me for granted as your partner and do very little creative partnering."

"Alright, I hear that. I'm going to work on it. I still want to know if you've been having an affair."

"I haven't. But it doesn't mean I haven't thought about it—not about an affair in particular, but meeting someone else. It's lonely being married to you, Richard."

I was hard-pressed for words.

"What are you feeling?" Gellert asked me.

"I feel sad—more for Karen than myself. For myself, I feel like a failure."

No one said anything.

"Richard," Karen said after a few moments, "I never told you because it wasn't important. I did have lunch with Daniels after that cast party. You and I were just beginning to date, and I wasn't sure how I felt about you. He asked me out, and I went."

"And?"

"And nothing. He was a nice guy. Kind of bohemian. He was very charming, but I felt more attracted to you."

"How so?"

"He made me laugh, but you gripped me at a deeper level."

"How so?"

"You were very solid. I admired your integrity. I remember being impressed by the fact that, considering you were an atheist, your moral values and sense of social responsibility were so strong. They weren't dependent on anything outside of you, but on your own inner conviction. In that regard, I've always felt you were very spiritual."

"How do you feel about me now?"

"I still love you, and if we can make it work, I'd like to try. I'm not asking you to jump over hoops. I just need to be with someone who is more attentive and interested in being married to *me*. I'm tired of feeling that I'm just a small part in your big picture."

"I understand."

After some probing by Gellert about what precisely I understood—I talked about my need to be more sensitive to Karen and her needs—he asked Karen for her associations to Teilhard de Chardin.

"I don't really have any," she said. "I know he's a great thinker, but I never read anything by him. I didn't know that Richard had such disdain for him. They're obviously on opposite ends of the spectrum in evolutionary science. However, I should say that one of the things Marc said to me over lunch was that he had been reading Teilhard and considered him his spiritual grandfather. He said he could read him in the original French because he had been born in France and had spent his early years there. It's funny how I don't remember much of anything we talked about, but I do remember that."

"*Really!?*" I asked Karen with astonishment. "He said Teilhard was his spiritual grandfather and that he was born in France?"

"Yes. I didn't know that either. His English was perfect," she said, glancing at Gellert.

"Is that cryptomnesia, too?" Gellert asked me. Karen looked perplexed.

"Hidden memories," I said to her. "When you think you're learning something for the first time but in fact learned it before but forgot about it." Turning to Gellert, I said, "It's an interesting coincidence. But it's not the same thing. In the vision, he's his godfather."

"True. Nevertheless, both terms have religious connotations."

"It's still just a random coincidence. Tell me," I said to Karen, "have you heard anything about Daniels since grad school?"

"No. I thought after reading your experience I might give Cathy Moynihan a call and ask her about him. I haven't spoken to her in years." Cathy Moynihan was Karen's college friend who introduced her to Daniels.

"What do you make of your own role in the vision?" Gellert asked Karen. "I'm referring particularly to the discussion about the Apocalypse."

"It intrigued me. I never studied the Apocalypse as a distinct theme in Renaissance literature, but it was always there as a strong influence. Not only on Milton, but on Shakespeare, Boccaccio, and Spenser. As for the connection to modern times, I can't speak about Teilhard's views, but many of the things my character said in the vision about a coming transformation of global consciousness are sentiments close to my heart. In fact, I'd like to reread some of these Renaissance authors in light of this connection."

"Michael thinks the Apocalypse theme also reflects my own psychological state," I said. "The surgery, our separation, the problems with Rachel and Ben, my depression, have all come together as an expression of the Apocalypse archetype, a personal death and rebirth."

Karen put her hand on my arm and said, "That might not be such a bad thing, sweetheart. The French word *Renaissance* literally refers to the rebirth of European culture after the Middle Ages, which included the Dark Ages. Look at all the beautiful things that came with that rebirth. And what did Goethe say, that without inner dying and coming to life again, we're only a gloomy guest on this dark Earth?"

"Well, that's exactly how I feel, like a gloomy guest on this dark Earth. I have no idea what a rebirth would look like."

"I know you've been in darkness and pain," Karen said, squeezing my arm. "Maybe some good will come out of it."

We sat quietly, each of us seemingly reflecting upon our own private thoughts. For myself, I thought about how I had here become what I understood clinical psychology to mean by the "identified patient," the one with the problems. I didn't like it.

"Karen," Gellert said at last, "you likened Richard's experience to Paul's on the road to Damascus. Can you say a little more about this?"

"Paul was an ironclad skeptic in the religious context of his day. So is Richard. It took a vision of Jesus for Paul to break out of his skepticism. Maybe this experience will compel Richard to reconsider all that he has shut out."

"Why do you imagine he has shut it out?"

"I'm sure his upbringing has a lot to do with it. I think the death of his sister broke the spirit of his family."

"You'd like this experience to convert me into a believer like Paul's did with him, wouldn't you?" I said to Karen.

"Richard, I really don't care whether or not you believe in the 'evidence of things unseen,' as Paul would say. I don't love you because of what you believe. But it would be a welcome change if this experience opened your mind a little, if you had at least some sense of wonder about it before quickly condemning it as an aberration. Your sense of conviction, which I admire even if I don't always agree with it, is one thing, but your smugness is another. That has been there since I've known you, and has gotten even worse over the years. You were smug even with Teilhard de Chardin. A great man who many consider a modern-day prophet appeared to you in a vision, invited you into his home as his guest, and you treated him, in your own words, like a pontificating phantom. Even if he were only a hallucination, couldn't you have been a little more gracious in the face of such mystery? I know you were under the stress of brain surgery, but really, how often does one get an experience like that? I envy you, Richard. I wish I had such an experience."

In the end, I was utterly alone. Unlike Karen and Gellert, I could find no spiritual solace in an experience that offered as evidence of things unseen only things seen in a state whose existence apart from the mind has no evidence. What is that state, after all?

Seventh Appointment
The Burning Center

I took a week off before my next session with Gellert
so I could better absorb all that was discussed in the
meeting with Karen. Due to events that occurred during
this week, I went into his office highly charged. I was
so flooded and yet on fire that I phoned ahead and
requested a double session.

"Michael, I have a real problem," I said at the outset
of our meeting. "It began with a dream, the most vivid
dream I've ever had. It was like an epic." He was listening
attentively. I unfolded a few sheets of paper on which I
had written the dream down, and began to read aloud.

*I am on top of a peak in Tibet. It is not the peak of a
mountain but rather the top of a huge pillar, spear-
tipped like a stalagmite and consisting entirely of stone.
A Buddhist temple or monastery has been built out
of the stone, so that it caps the pillar and is an integral part of it. I am here with two men, one a Sherpa
guide who brought me here and the other a tourist like
myself. They leave me here, as the guide is going to
bring the other tourist to another temple some miles*

away. Across the way, just a couple of hundred yards, is another jutting peak, with no temple on top. I could see three Westerners climbing it with ropes. I implicitly understand that this temple has been abandoned, and that the Chinese government has granted these climbers, the other tourist, and myself special visas to come here. For some reason, one of the climbers has his ropes anchored into the pillar I am on in case he falls. The other climbers' ropes are nailed into the pillar they're climbing. I look down the extraordinary geological formation whose stone steps I had evidently climbed to get up here, and it is a long way down. I am on top of the world. Stone peaks similar to this one surround it and fill the horizon. They are awesome.

I am in a small courtyard in front of the entrance into the temple, near the edge of the peak. A man comes out of the temple. It is Daniels. Dressed as a Tibetan Buddhist monk, he is wearing a yellow vest with a red robe and a long red cape that is flapping in the wind. He greets me and says he has been waiting for me. He asks if I would like to take a look at the cosmos of the plane he lives in. I say yes. We walk over to the edge of the cliff and look upon the exquisite rockscape all around us. Then, as if a curtain is drawn open, a multitude of stars crystallizes against a vast black background. But they are not like those in the ordinary night sky. They are organized in clusters that look like trees of various kinds, sizes, and densities. Many have shapely branches stretching out in all directions, giving them a stately quality. Some are tall and slim like Italian cypress trees, others have a widespread canopy like the acacias on the savan-

nas of Africa, and yet others look like cactus trees. The expanse of dark, empty space surrounding the trees gives an impression of black soil. Though the trees stand separately with sizeable distances between them, together they appear as a forest, as a single, interrelated cosmic organism. The sight of them as far as the eye could see is breathtaking.

Looking carefully at a nearby tree, I see that its flickering lights are not really stars at all. Their slight movements make the tree appear alive with activity. Their ensemble emits a strange, soothing, melodic hum that penetrates the core of my being. With both masculine and feminine elements, it is as if every musical note were being sounded harmoniously at the same time.

"Each tree is a heaven," Daniels says. "And in each heaven are the spiritual essences of the people inhabiting it, the flashing lights you see. Look how vibrant those spiritual essences are in their togetherness, and how many different niches they can inhabit. Each niche is a different pocket of activity. Like the physical world, all this is in flux and evolving. Come."

Somehow I am no longer in my body. I am moving in the sky as a pure essence, as light. It is an exhilarating feeling. Sensing Daniels beside me—he is a light too—I know he is pulling me along. Inside my mind, he says, "Consider this an astral Garden of Eden." With a tremendous but effortless speed, we shoot into space, gliding around one tree after the other. "Over there is the Christian heaven," Daniels says as we approach an enormous tree. It is majestic, with so many branches that I don't think I could count them. It takes a while to make a *partial arc around it, and then even more time as we go toward another tree.*

As we come up toward a different tree, Daniels says, "There is the Islamic heaven." And it is also magnificent. As we traverse great distances, Daniels identifies the heavens of other Western and Eastern religions—the Jewish heaven pulsating with a brilliance that makes up for its smaller size. Even smaller are all the other trees that far outnumber those of the few major religions. Daniels names a number of them. I am familiar with only a few. They are not religions but societies or collectives of different kinds. "There are the Rosicrucians," he says. "And there, the existentialists. Over there, the Transcendentalists and Romantics. And there's a society that one day you'll probably want to visit: Darwin, Lamarck, and their intellectual descendants. Here they are studying the evolution of everything you see."

And then I notice—though I recognize they've been there all along—slight flashes of spritely movement between the trees. As if reading my mind, Daniels says, "People move between the worlds. No heaven is an island unto itself. Each tree is a unique community of purpose working on what is important to it. Its people share what Tibetan Buddhists call a karmic vision. But people can also dwell in multiple communities, and more or less simultaneously."

"Let's go back," Daniels says after a few moments. We continue in an arc and approach a tree we hadn't seen, apparently, I now gather, because it is where we started from. "That is the Buddhist heaven," he says.

We zoom into a sector of it, and then into a sector within that sector, and finally approach a bright spherical light. All at once I find myself in my body again, standing in front of the temple, in complete silence except for the blowing wind. The immense vista of trees is replaced by a dark sky whose stars are hardly visible because there is a full moon. Daniels is to my side. In the moonlight I can see the climbers on the adjacent peak. In the time that has passed they have climbed higher.

Daniels says, "Do you want to know what Pierre said to Karen when I was making coffee and you were too tired to listen?" I say yes. "He told her that evolution can be fully understood only in light of the burning center. Do you know what that might be?" I say no. "Look for it in his letters," he says. "It is the secret of evolution, and also the key to your marriage. Now you should go down below. Your better half is waiting for you." I look at the stairs to which he points. When I look back, he is gone.

I go to the stairs and begin to descend. Time seems compressed and I quickly arrive at the bottom, at a meadow amidst the towering pillars that surround it, four of them in full view from where I stand. The meadow, far below their peaks, is lush with palm trees and tropical plants and flowers. A shallow, gurgling stream meanders through the meadow between the towers. The soft light of the moon, which is visible just above one of the peaks, is funneled down between these four peaks. Because it is rebounding off their stone walls, it is almost radiant. I have never seen such a beautiful place.

*I see Karen on a picnic blanket by the stream. I am
happy to see her. With a wave of her arm, she motions me
to come over. Intuitively I know it is my Karen, not his.*

*On the blanket is a spread of food, mostly fruit—
mangos, pomegranate, passion fruit, bananas, coconut. I
sit down, and we eat, not speaking a word.*

*Across the stream there is a rustling sound. An ani-
mal emerges from some bushes. At first it appears to be
a wolf. Then it looks more like a panther. It sees us and
slowly begins to cross the stream, heading in our direction. I'm frightened. I stand up and try to pull Karen
up by her arm, but she does not respond. As the animal gets closer I realize it is unlike anything I've ever
seen. It has a shiny black, furry body. Its face is white
with a long-bridged ruby-red nose and flaring nostrils
like what mandrill monkeys have. It has a small oval
mouth and chin. Bright yellow streaks run down the
sides of its head to its neck. Between its bulging, beady
eyes is a leaf-like growth of some kind, also yellow. I
try to* whoosh! *it away, but it keeps coming toward
us. It stops about midway across the stream. It stands
up on its two hind legs, looking now like a kangaroo.
It is staring intently at me. I see it has a penis. Yet it
also has female breasts, much like a human or other
primate. At that instant, like a lizard, its neck expands
to twice its previous girth, and a loud, throaty noise
bellows out of its mouth or nostrils. It sounds like the
blowing of a galloping horse or the flapping wings of a
large bird. The thing drops back down on its fours and
starts moving toward us again. I'm scared out of my
wits.* What does it want? *I look at Karen. She turns*

her gaze towards me. Again, that Mona Lisa counte-
nance. She is not afraid. *I look back at the creature. It*
is about eight feet away. I awaken.

I looked up from my notes at Gellert. I waited for his
response for what seemed like a long time. Finally, he
said, "So what's your problem?"

"I'll tell you my problem," I said. "I don't have a
problem with this dream. It's just as crazy as my vision,
if not crazier. If I could live with one, I could live with
the other. What I have a problem with is what happened
after the dream."

I then told Gellert that I had decided to take up Daniels's challenge to search for the burning center—the
secret of evolution and the key to my marriage—in Teilhard's letters. As I could find nothing on the Internet, I
went to my university's library. There were ten volumes
of his letters spanning fifty years of his life. I searched
through them for the words "burning center," until I
came upon one volume consisting of letters exclusively
to two friends living in America. An obscure book, it's
called *Letters to Two Friends*. I carefully looked through it
too. And there, in the book's prologue and repeated in
the final letter to one of these friends, I found the passage I was looking for. Having brought the book with
me, I opened it to the passage and read it, too, out loud
to Gellert. Teilhard's words were about the sense of confidence and surrender we should all feel for the "vast
and powerful movement of the Universe which, at first
approximation, is a 'process' in the eyes of science, but
which upon the *complete* study of Man reveals itself as

necessarily belonging to the species of a Life and even of a Love. Not the 'black pit,' but the burning center, whatever it is."

"Michael," I said, "the burning center is a species of life and love that Teilhard insinuates is God. *That's* what Daniels was referring to in my dream. Naturally, I went home in a state of shock. To be sure this wasn't a case of cryptomnesia, I decided to reread the two books by Teilhard that I read as a graduate student—*The Phenomenon of Man* and *The Future of Man*. I am certain that I have not read anything else by him."

"And?" Gellert said. "Did you find any references to the burning center in them?"

I explained that I did not. Teilhard speaks of the centricity of energy and of organisms as centers of life and consciousness, he speaks of psychic centration or involution, and he even speaks of the Omega as the "mysterious centre of our centres" and as an "ever-warmer radiance," but he does not mention a burning center.

"So what's your problem?" Gellert said.

"My problem is that there's no way that information could have gotten into my head. Its first appearance was in my dream, and the precise reference to its source in Teilhard's letters is not something I had any knowledge about. This was not a case of cryptomnesia."

"Why is that a problem?"

"*BECAUSE IT'S SCIENTIFICALLY IMPOSSIBLE!*"

"Why are you shouting?"

"Because either you're not hearing me or you're playing with me! *It suggests that the dream world is connected to the physical world!*"

"Yes, that's exactly what it suggests. Is the problem that the two worlds are connected or that you cannot accept that they are connected?"

"Michael, it's not just me who cannot accept they are connected. The entire scientific establishment cannot accept they are connected."

"Well, evidently you just had an experience that is not acceptable to the entire scientific establishment. Maybe you have more in common with Teilhard than you think."

I stared at him.

"Michael," I said, "how is this possible?"

He stared back. After some moments, he got up and went over to one of the bookcases in his office. He looked about for some book, pulled one out, came back to his chair, and leafed through it. Finally finding what he was looking for, he read aloud: "If a man could pass through Paradise in a dream, and have a flower presented to him as a pledge that his soul had really been there, and if he found that flower in his hand when he awoke—Ay! And what then?" He then looked up at me and said, "Coleridge. Did you know that his poem, *Kubla Khan*, was envisioned in a dream? He said that he forgot most of it before he could write it all down. As it was, the fragment he retrieved is one of the masterpieces of English literature."

"Yes, he was a talented opium addict. I ask you again, how is this possible?"

"Do you mean how can it be explained?"

"Yes."

"Numerous ways, but I doubt you will find any of them scientifically provable. They cannot be subjected to the scientific method and their hypotheses cannot be repeatedly demonstrated by experiment. Though I imagine the ancients who devised such divination systems as astrology and the *I Ching* might disagree with that. In any case, one way to explain how dream states can connect with the physical world is Leibniz's doctrine of preestablished harmony. It asserts that the mental and the material consist of two different kinds of substance that act in concert because they have been programmed to do so as part of creation. Jung, looking for a less vague understanding of how synchronistic experiences like yours could happen, built upon the psychoid factor of early psychologists like Hans Driesch and Eugen Bleuler. He theorized that the deepest layer of the unconscious, well below the personal and collective unconscious, is psychoid, meaning that it is *like* the psyche, but not quite the psyche. It imperceptibly merges with the body and its autonomic nervous system—everything that keeps the body running and that we do not, for the large part, consciously control. However, by virtue of this, the psychoid layer also merges with the same material world whose primordial molecules and atoms the body itself is composed of. It is the common root of both psyche and matter. This is a radical theory, that the unconscious extends beyond the psyche."

"How exactly does this explain my experience?"

"If the psyche is highly charged, it can, via this psychoid layer, briefly cross over into the physical realm, thus making it possible to connect the letter mentioned in your dream with the actual letter published in a book. That is what synchronicity is—an event in which

the inner and outer worlds are connected by the psychoid factor. Jung here not only resolved the ancient
mind-body or spirit-matter problem, in which the two
sides were split apart, but he introduced the psyche
into Einstein's space-time continuum. By connecting
the psyche with this continuum, the psychoid factor
creates a greater whole that bends the usual laws and
boundaries of nature and makes paranormal occurrences possible."

"All that this theory does is cleverly insert a connecting third agent into the mind-matter equation. What
proof is there that this really exists?"

Leaning in close, Gellert bore into me with his eyes.
"Richard," he said, "the experience you just had is the
proof. It's not going to get better than that. You can question and explore the theory, and maybe even come up
with a better one, but if in the end you can't accept the
living proof of your own experience, you should just forget about it and move on."

He then slammed the Coleridge book shut, got up,
and put it back in its place on the bookshelf. Returning
to his seat, he said, "I'm afraid you are so caught up in
the logistics of this event that you are missing the dimension of its meaning. Pray tell, *what does it mean to you* that
a species of love—thus, *love itself*—is the secret of evolution and the key to your marriage?"

"I can accept the part about the marriage, but not
about evolution. The idea that love is a cosmic force
binding the elements of the universe together goes back
to the early natural philosophers—Empedocles in particular. It's prescientific."

185

"So you can accept the part about your marriage? It didn't seem that way in our last meeting with Karen."

"What do you mean?"

"She expressed a number of times that she loved you and showed genuine affection even though she was critical. All you were able to muster up was that you had feelings for her. I'm not saying that as a rule you had to return her affections and confess your love, but it struck me how you were much more emotional about Karen in the session before when you were here alone with me. Is it hard for you to express your love to her?"

"I felt a little guarded."

"About what?"

"I wasn't sure where I stood with her."

"Yes you were. She made it quite clear. What are you afraid of?"

I was unable to answer.

"Are you afraid of the intensity of your own feelings?" he asked.

"You're referring to the animal?"

"Answer the question."

We sat quietly.

"What are you feeling right now?" Gellert asked.

"I don't know. I'm uncomfortable."

"Stay with it."

We sat quietly.

"When my sister died," I said after a minute or so, "my family shut down. It was so painful, nobody could talk about it. In a way, I felt like my brother and I were taking care of our parents by *not* talking about it. But pretending that her absence wasn't there only made it more glaring. I think I'm afraid that if I really loved again the way I loved Alison, and let myself feel it, if I lost the person the pain would be unbearable. With my kids I somehow manage to tolerate this discomfort, maybe because they're dependent on me. But with Karen, I've been afraid to love her that deeply. I don't want to be that dependent on her."

"Dependency needs are human, Richard. Being overdependent or codependent is a problem, but being afraid of basic dependency needs can be just as much a problem. It shuts down intimacy and kills love. Look at yourself: you have a wife who loves you and whom you love, but you're afraid to fall in love with her. Do you know that's one thing you left out each time we spoke about your relationship? You never said you fell in love with her. Did you?"

"Yes."

"Did she know that?"

"I would think so."

"Did you tell her?"

"No, not as such. But why is that important? I thought therapists of the psychoanalytic persuasion don't believe in falling in love, that it's just a projection."

"I'm talking about the enchantment of love itself, not the euphoria of fusion. That's projection. But even if that were your experience, isn't that the way we initially come to know anything, by first identifying with it in our imagination and attributing to it the things we want it to be? Falling in love is just a beginning. Again, if you make something *just* a projection without following up on the larger reality it points to, you risk reducing it to its most simple elements. However, that's not the point here. It's important because if you never told her how you felt, how do you know it was ever *shared*? I'd be the first to tell you that not everything needs to be expressed in words, but in your case I'm wondering if it was ever expressed at all."

"What does this have to do with my dream?"

"Maybe nothing, maybe everything. I'm not so concerned here with your dream."

"*Oh really?* I thought dreams are very important to you."

"There's a saying in the Talmud, 'Don't let the dream be bigger than the night.'"

"Well, this dream *was* bigger than the night. In fact, it has overshadowed my days as well. That's what I want to talk about right now."

"Okay, then talk about your dream."

"No," I said. "I'm tired of this psychoanalytic game of hide-and-seek. I don't have a clue what this dream is about and I want you to tell me."

"Are you angry at me?"

"Michael, I've hardly slept in three nights. The other day I had to ask Karen to keep the kids on what should have been my night with them. I'm too agitated to see them. I'm not in the mood for this. I'm ready to walk out that door any moment."

"Richard, if I tell you what the dream means, what are you going to do with that information? It's the same question Teilhard asked you. If here too you are compelled to reduce your paranormal experience with Teilhard's letter to some scientifically provable explanation, what are you going to do with the burning center of the universe that is also at the center of your dream?"

"Let me worry about that. It's not your problem."

We stared at each other, each waiting for the other to blink.

"Alright," he said. "Let's talk about your dream. It's a profound dream. You could spend your whole life working on it and I'm sure you'd always find new meanings. The dream portrays the problem of your life and is coming to help you with that, if you can receive it. It is showing you the scheme of evolution as the *psyche* sees it while at the same time telling you about your personal evolution, about what needs to happen in your life. Let's start at the beginning. What are your associations with Tibet?"

I could see he was not going to give away the store, and I was afraid that what I was secretly storing would arm him even more.

"I have something else to add to all this, Michael. The morning after I had this dream, Karen called me to tell me she had reached her friend Cathy and had inquired about Daniels. He died four years ago. It was a freak accident. He had become an off-Broadway director in New York. He was married to an actress and had two girls, one from his wife's former marriage and the other from theirs. He came out of their loft in SoHo one night and was walking to a nearby grocery store when a car being chased by the police suddenly turned down the street he was on. The car went onto the sidewalk and ran right into him, throwing him against a building. He died instantly. It reminded me of my sister."

"My goodness!" Gellert said.

"That's not all. Daniels had become a serious practitioner of Tibetan Buddhism. This was well after our college days. Again, there was no way I could have known that. After this I decided to go to the library and research Teilhard's letters."

"So there are two synchronicities here," Gellert said. "One with Teilhard, the other with Daniels."

We sat quietly. Describing these irrational experiences to Gellert somehow gave them more weight, as if hearing myself talk and having a witness further validated them. Now they were out in the world and not just private events. And yet I still could not fully believe them myself.

"Let's come back to the question," Gellert said. "What are your associations with Tibet?"

"The typical ones. Clearly, the Tibetans are a spiritual people. One can only feel compassion for their plight."

"Which is?"

"They're in exile because the Chinese drove them out."

"So perhaps you were visiting a place in the psyche from which *you* are in exile because you've been driven out by some tyrannical ruling principle. What might that be?"

"You'd like me to say that it's the scientific method or logic, wouldn't you?"

"When you try to force a paranormal dream such as this into a scientific framework that cannot sufficiently explain it, then I would say the scientific method or logic has become tyrannical. Even Freud eventually acknowledged the mysterious nature of paranormal phenomena. Your one-sided materialism is, in a different form, the state religion of China, dialectical materialism. But again, look at what the dream may be asking of you. It seems that for some reason you've been given a visa. An exception or privilege has been granted on your behalf to visit a mysterious land dominated by an occupying force. You have a choice, Richard, take it or leave it. If you take it, new vistas may open for you, as in the cosmos Daniels unveiled and gave you a tour of. If you don't take it, you'll probably be here a year from now still advocating the hegemony of the scientific method and logic."

"Michael, a week ago I would have dismissed everything you are saying. I may not yet be able to wholeheartedly accept the living proof of my paranormal experience, but I can't deny it either. I can't sleep because the basic order of the cosmos as I've known it has just been turned upside down. The dream world has just proven to me that it is as real as the physical world. I don't have any intellectual model or framework for that, other than what you've given me. To you, this may seem normal. To me, it's not."

"I know that, Richard. I may lean heavily on the viewpoint of the unconscious, but I'm on your side. I can appreciate how tough this is for you. In your vision Karen mentioned Doris Lessing. I am reminded of something she wrote in regard to paranormal phenomena, that people don't believe in them until they experience them. Then when they experience them they become people that other people don't believe."

I suppose I now had to accept that I had just joined the ranks of people whom other people disbelieve on account of their paranormal experiences. Or, as Gellert suggested, I've even joined the ranks of Teilhard. If I were to divulge my experience to my colleagues, not only in the field of evolutionary psychology but psychology at large, I'd become an outcast. As a Jungian, Gellert himself was an outcast.

"What are your associations with Tibetan Buddhism in particular?" Gellert asked.

"All I can think of is its ideas on reincarnation and bardos, which I learned about from Karen. I know *The Tibetan Book of the Dead* is one of its main scriptures. I understand that it describes a complicated process of what supposedly happens after we die."

"Yes. The bardos are different states of consciousness that include both the one we're in and the dream bardo, which according to this tradition you visited in your dream, if not also your vision. The other bardos are mostly transitional phases between death and rebirth, and visions could also occur in some of them. On the whole, I think it's safe to say that the Tibetan Buddhist imagery in your dream points to your own death and rebirth, psychologically speaking."

"This cosmos, is it actually discussed in Tibetan Buddhism?"

"No more than there are Tibetan monasteries carved out of stone on huge stalagmites. It seems to be a distinct innovation of the unconscious."

"Have you ever heard of one like it?"

"No."

"You said before that the dream is showing me the scheme of evolution as the psyche sees it. If that is the case, there must be accounts similar to this in the annals of religious experience."

"There are plenty of accounts of visionary and near-death experiences involving visits to astral worlds, both in the West and the East. Some are similar to each other and some not. Generally, they may be seen as the psyche's *allusions* to what is beyond. There's a big difference between an allusion and an illusion. Such anecdotal visits to other worlds may not be literal representations, but rather the psyche's own images of the wholeness it is evolving toward. These are images of the higher self no less than a figure like Teilhard, except they are cosmic rather than personified. They are also the psyche's way of saying that something continues beyond this existence. As Jung observed, our dreams treat death purely as a physical occurrence and not the final end. Here too Daniels reports that people continue to work on what's important to them in these reconstituted, heavenly communities. He reinforces what was discussed in your vision—that the cosmos is evolving at different levels. Whether or not this is literal, and in the particular way it's portrayed, who can say with absolute certainty? But as an allusion, it's very telling. The cosmos of the *psyche* continues to evolve."

"In our meeting before last you suggested that dreams of the dead can be actual visitations—what did Jung say? 'The dead are standing directly behind us.' How could you have made that statement if here you are claiming that these dreams are just images from the psyche?"

"Again, you are minimizing the reality of the psyche. They're not *just* images. They're allusions. Whatever the afterlife is, it is probably *in* the psyche or *of* the psyche no less than anything else in your dreams. The question is, do we continue to exist in some form after the body dies, going into the living psyche like we go into it every night in our dreams?"

"Do we?"

"'I sent my Soul through the Invisible, / Some letter of that After-life to spell: / And by and by my Soul return'd to me, / And answer'd "I Myself am Heav'n and Hell."' That's one of my favorite lines from *The Rubaiyat of Omar Khayyam.* I don't think Khayyam was merely waxing poetic here. He was being psychological, deeply psychological. And he was no opium addict."

"I'm still unclear. Are you saying that Daniels here is a figure from the psyche or that he is actually visiting me from the afterlife?"

"I'm *not* saying. It's a mystery, isn't it, how realities beyond the everyday mind may act or act together, or how they may be different and yet the same?"

"Are you playing with me again, Michael?"

"I'm not playing with you at all. Who can say with absolute certainty whether the likeness of Daniels in your dream is not somehow shaped by something on the other side of this life? It is true that on the one hand he is portrayed here as a kind of mythical, Orpheus figure who can visit the afterworld and even comes from it, and that he is again in the archetypal role of guide. Indeed, it didn't seem like he was standing behind you waiting for your answer to some question of human destiny, but rather was providing you with answers. The dead rarely come to visit us with this kind of mission. Mediumistic experiences in which the dead supposedly reveal cosmic truths and divine plans for humanity tend to be dreamlike phenomena of the unconscious—not to be dismissed, but not to be taken literally either. When the dead do appear to authentically provide answers, these are usually in regard to some unfinished business with the person they're visiting. So in all these regards Daniels seems to be an agent of the living psyche. On the other hand, I wouldn't be so quick to assume that all this rules out possibilities that are simply incomprehensible in our present, limited condition. How the fabric of the world is woven across multiple realms, tying together different threads, is an age-old source of wonder to mystics and shamans. Who knows what condition Daniels is in today, or for that matter, Teilhard, and what trace residues or elements of their psyches found their way into your dream and vision?"

"So you mean to tell me that based on such truly incomprehensible vagaries you believe we survive death, is that right?"

"I believe *something* survives, if not the ego as we know it. And no, that's not the basis of my belief, just a hypothesis."

"Then what do you base it on?"

"Richard, as you've mentioned you know, I trained with a Zen master in Japan. I've also had many years of Jungian analysis myself. I have no difficulty honoring what I've learned from these experiences."

"What have you learned?"

"I learned that things are not all that they appear to be, and that there are things that don't appear at all."

"Can you be more explicit?"

"No."

195

"You're not going to tell me anything about yourself, are you?"

"No, I'm not. You have enough going on in your own psyche to deal with right now. Besides, it wouldn't help you. Trust me."

"Then do you have any other interpretations of this revelation of an afterlife in my dream, perhaps something more down-to-earth?"

"Yes, as a matter of fact, I do. It's conceivable that this higher cosmos is also a symbolic image of what a new social order could be like in *this* world. After all, the tale this dream tells is spun on the loom of the Apocalypse archetype no less than your vision. We should not forget that this archetype is about the death and rebirth of the world we actually inhabit, whether we are speaking on an individual or a global level. All those different collective trees rooted in a common garden and connected by shooting lights could be a new world order that the psyche is championing *here* if not in the afterlife. This garden could also simply be an image that the collective unconscious is providing of itself, that of a consortium or storehouse of all the world's religious knowledge."

"That's a little more palatable. Though I do have to admit that the dream seemed so real. I felt I was really there, gliding through space amidst these illustrious trees."

"You were. Remember Jung's patient on the moon. That same moon was in your dream."

"Let's talk about that. What was that event with Karen about?"

"Good question. What do you make of it?"

"Could the descent down the stairs be a metaphor for the topography of the mind—the unconscious being down below?"

"Yes, certainly. The Tibetan Buddhist temple or monastery on top of a peak, the metaphysical cosmos Daniels revealed to you—these reflect the spiritual heights and the enlightened consciousness we are evolving towards. *God.* The lush meadow below, the picnic with Karen and its tropical fruits, the strange animal—these give voice to nature and the psyche's depths. What makes us *human.* The world above is the mind and spirit—rational, suprarational, and cosmic. The world below is the heart and soul—often irrational, but always related to who we are as *persons.* As you said, that was *your* Karen, not his. There she sits on the ground floor of your being, feasting silently and holding the secret key to your marriage and evolution. The movement down is very important. Above we find our divinity, but below, our humanity. Now, what do you make of that full moon, funneling its soft light down between the peaks?"

"I don't know. It had a magical quality."

"Yes, that's the magic of the soul. Lunar consciousness. The spiritual worlds above operate under the auspices of solar consciousness—the higher self. But lunar consciousness rules the night, with its twilight world of magical creatures and its dark mysteries of nature."

"I must confess, Michael, sometimes I think you make these things up as you go along."

He laughed. "No, unfortunately my personal imagination isn't wild enough for that. This is all from the archetypal imagination. Your entire dream is archetypally structured and nuanced, and not just with its apocalyptic theme or Daniels's role as a guide. For instance, it is no mere coincidence that you descend from Tibetan Buddhism into the passions of the soul and the body, into the anima and animal within you. As Jung pointed out, *The Tibetan Book of the Dead* begins with the highest state of consciousness occurring at the moment of death. Consciousness then increasingly degrades, finally concluding with a new physical birth. The transformation goes from the spiritual to the physical, from higher to lower. This is reverse to the transformation process usually pictured in the West. In *The Egyptian Book of the Dead*, Plato's myth of Er, and the New Testament, the soul advances to a more refined spiritual existence. Your dream is similar to the Tibetan Buddhist view in that your evolution is illustrated as a descent into an earlier, more primitive form. It's important that you get this on a gut level, Richard, that you understand how your personal salvation lies in the animal realm—in *feeling with passion*, for example, the love you profess you have for your wife. 'Be a good animal, true to your animal instincts,' D. H. Lawrence said. Tell me, when was the last time you made love to Karen?"

His question caught me off-guard. "It has been a while. Our love life became empty and flat as our marriage deteriorated over the last few years."

"Of course—there's no surprise there. But it's not only your sex life calling for the animal. The entire marriage needs it. The heart is both physical and spiritual, both animal and godly. The *ortus* is a most godly animal."

"The *what*?"

"You saw an ortus. It's a magical animal, like the unicorn or dragon. Like all animals in the dream or mythical world, it embodies the instinctual, primitive side of the higher self or God—*your* instinctual, primitive side, including the passion and love you are afraid of but, as the dream illustrated, Karen is not. The seventeenth-century European alchemist Michael Maier wrote about the ortus based on anecdotes he heard while traveling in Africa near the Red Sea. He thought that the ortus was the phoenix, another magical animal. He knew that the crossing of the Red Sea by the Israelites was a death-and-rebirth experience, so he naturally assumed that the magical creature reported in this region was the phoenix. So you could say that an underlying meaning of the ortus, at least in the European imagination, is the phoenix, just like an underlying meaning of the image of Galileo is Copernicus. But that's only one association and, in fact, the ortus is *not* the phoenix but a creature in its own right. Your ortus appears different than the one Maier heard about, but that is of little significance with a creature who is probably a shape-shifter. Also different, yours is a hermaphrodite. Because it unites the opposites of both genders, Jung described the hermaphrodite as it appears in mythology as a subduer of conflicts and a bringer of healing. However, very much like Maier's ortus, yours bears the four primary colors of alchemy—black, white, yellow, and red. These colors correspond to the stages involved in turning lead into gold."

"*Alchemy?*" I said, astonished. This was the second time Gellert raised this subject. The predecessor of modern chemistry, alchemy persisted as late as with Newton, who wisely kept his occult experiments a secret. By the turn of the nineteenth century, alchemy had been swept into the dustbin of history as irrational hocus-pocus.

"Yes," Gellert said. "Inherent within alchemy is a psychology of personal development, best understood through its symbolism. The alchemists projected psychological processes of transformation into matter. Jung understood their concrete pursuit of changing lead or other crude substances into gold in terms of the stages of self-realization."

"How do the colors correspond to this?"

"Black is connected with lead, white with silver, yellow with gold, and red with the consummation of the entire process. Lead is the *prima materia* or *massa confusa*, the initial state of chaos in the psyche—the leaden, depressed condition that brought you here. When whitened, it becomes pure. One becomes free of false attachments and ideas about oneself. Silver represents the moon, the lunar consciousness in whose luminescence the nature of the psyche and one's own nature are clarified. You could say you've been working on that here. Gold is a symbol of the sun or solar consciousness and the higher self, whose realization is the goal of individuation. I imagine this may be what you are working towards. However, gold attains its greatest value when it becomes red, the color of blood, emotion, and instinct, including not only the human but also the animal dimension. Without the passion of redness, gold is just another inert metal. Thus, red signifies the marriage of the sun and moon, or the divine and the human. It is the most complete form of self-realization because it brings God into the human sphere.

So, you see, your dream portrays not only the Buddhist idea of evolution, but also the alchemical one. The ortus represents the animal aspect of the higher self. Its emergence out of the unconscious, out of the bushes, calls for a realization of God—viscerally, not just intellectually—that includes your animal nature. *Your dream hints at a royal marriage between the solar and lunar worlds and the divine and animal dimensions within you. This* is the secret key to your marriage and evolution."

Gellert's interpretation was so absurd that I wondered if any other could possibly make sense of such an absurd dream. I quizzed him further about the symbolic underpinnings of my dream. He explained how the stone pillars in my dream may allude to the "philosopher's stone," an elusive substance that represents wisdom and is the Holy Grail of alchemy. He said he wondered if the Western mountain climbers and the ropes between the two stone peaks signify the growing connection between Western and Eastern wisdom. He also mentioned the "Axiom of Maria," a principle of transformation discovered by a female Jewish alchemist in Egypt—possibly the founder of Western alchemy—in the third century. It emerges in the curious play on numbers in the dream: myself to begin with, then the two men I came to the temple with, the three mountain climbers, and the four pillars surrounding the meadow. He said that this points towards a new state of awareness that integrates the various opposites splitting me apart—mind and heart, matter and spirit, science and religion, instinct and thought, eros and logos, masculine and feminine. These riddle my conflicts with Karen, Daniels, Teilhard, and, clearly, the ortus.

"It's no accident," he said, "that you woke up just before the ortus could reach you. You saw the likeness of Pan, and you panicked. This is the juncture you are at in your psychological process. Now you have to decide where you want to go with this, what you want to do with all this information. The rest of the dream—its conclusion and resolution—has to be lived consciously. Embrace the divine animal within you, Richard, and you'll not only be able to sleep peacefully again, but you'll truly awaken."

Postlude
A Capacity We All Possess

Until recently, I never truly understood what the playwright Gotthold Lessing meant when he said, "There are things which must cause you to lose your reason or you have none to lose." It is only reasonable, under circumstances such as mine, to lose your reason. My sense of reason itself—and not just its hypotheses and conclusions—had been hurled into Russell's condition of suspended judgment. The logic that had ordered my life up to now could no longer explain the things I was experiencing. Though somewhat esoteric, Gellert's explanations at least had an internal logic—a coherence and meaning, as he would say—that made sense within his framework.

In the period following my meeting with Gellert I read a number of Teilhard's works. His theories on the spiritual nature of evolution were no more provable than when I read them the first time, but they were also no more bizarre than the notion that the spiritual dream world exists with the same objective status as the material world. As that notion to me was now a fact, I read Teilhard's theories with new eyes. Perhaps they too were possible facts.

Certain conclusions became inescapable. To begin, evolutionary science cannot at present explain the paranormal experiences I had. In hindsight, it is likely that I had a series of them—the sweartshirt, pants, and Nikes my children gave me, identical to those in my vision; Daniels's interest in Teilhard (in the "real" world) and his French roots in both the visionary and real worlds; his connection to Tibetan Buddhism in both my dream and waking life; and of course, the presaged "burning center." Even the Unicum in my vision was probably something other than cryptomnesia. Such paranormal occurrences could not have happened unless there is a part of our mind that extends beyond our brain, connecting the inner psyche with the physical environment. Can this be the noosphere or psychoid layer of the unconscious?

There also seems to be some organizing agent or principle—a living psyche, a higher self, or some other phenomenon—that coordinates these occurrences. They are too specific—*too* coherent and meaningful—to be random accidents. They seem to be psychophysical wonders of a similar if not identical order as the physical wonders that prompted Einstein to famously say, "I do not believe that God plays dice with the universe." Does this extended part of our mind and its organizing principle belong to the process of evolution, or are they somehow independent of it, perhaps parallel to it yet intersecting it? Either way, evolutionary science has not yet begun to even recognize this mystery, much less solve it. When and if science makes the leap between the physical and spiritual worlds, proving that the latter exists with the same objective status as the former, there will be a scientific revolution or paradigm shift greater even than the Einsteinian one. It would be as significant a leap in human consciousness as the development of the rational, discursive ego that is the hallmark of civilization. It would probably also revolutionize our understanding of the mind-brain connection, resolving the ancient mind-body problem. Should this occur one day, Teilhard de Chardin and Jung might well be looked upon as its forerunners.

In my own small way I am increasingly undergoing this paradigm shift on a personal level. My original position, described at the outset of this story as an atheism that had no difficulty accepting religious experiences because it did not view them as outside the scope of natural phenomena, has changed. Because the scope of what constitutes "natural phenomena" has been enlarged by including a living psyche or higher self that meaningfully coordinates dreams, visions, and synchronicities, my understanding of "God" is more differentiated. My faith in the God of Aristotle, Spinoza, and Einstein—God as a cosmic principle, such as the First Principle that caused the universe to be born—has made way for a God that is also a psychic principle. It is no longer an abstract God but one whose workings I have witnessed in the experiences I have shared here. Although not a theological God, it is alive with numinous energy and the drive to get our attention so that we understand it as our most natural, even supernatural, endowment. God is a capacity we all possess.

If this paradigm shift has been going on within me in a small way, then the idea of the Apocalypse has had a huge impact. First conceived concretely in the Bible, the Apocalypse is understood psychologically and symbolically by Renaissance and modern thinkers alike. This psychological and symbolic understanding of the Apocalypse easily lends itself to the very concrete ecological events of our day—perhaps too easily—but it does bring it down to a very practical level. Our need to undergo an inner apocalypse—an inner death and rebirth—goes hand-in-hand with the increasing danger of an outer apocalypse, a planetary death or cataclysm. This danger is gaining momentum *daily*. Those of us who can open our eyes and see the mass extinction of species that is already occurring know that the global scientific community is not crying wolf when it warns us with alarm that we have only a limited amount of time to arrest the trend of climate change. *That* for sure is not a hallucination, even if you think—as I often did—that the anesthesia experience I've described in these pages is. If we fail to meet this ecological challenge, we risk crossing a threshold that will unravel the fine interrelatedness of biological life on this planet. Our global civilization may then unravel too, and even die, quite possibly with *billions* of people who live in it.

To repeat what I wrote earlier, there have been pre-historically at least five mass extinctions. If we think that a sixth one in the very near future—in our children's future if not our own—is merely a science-fiction fantasy or some distant problem, we are sorely mistaken. We have reason to fear that without a new mindset that prioritizes this issue above all others, we will sooner or later reach that threshold from which there will be no return. A major worldwide catastrophe would then be unavoidable. The psychological, sociopolitical, and economic changes that need to take place internationally to avert this are still far from being realized. We are too myopic, self-absorbed, and greedy in our drive to satisfy our appetites. Sacrifices, both collectively and individually, must be made in order to prevent global disaster. Replacing the industrial habits we've become addicted to with green alternatives would be a major undertaking, akin to but far surpassing the New Deal or the Marshall Plan. If we delay this much longer, I'm afraid that when we do face it, it will be too little too late. A viable response to climate change cannot occur in a climate of denial or postponement. I am not prone to hysterical apocalyptic thinking, certainly of the biblical kind, but if ever there were on this earth a likelihood of apocalyptic disaster on the same scale as previous mass extinctions and even Noah's flood, it is unfolding today before our very eyes.

To avoid a sixth mass extinction—possibly including *our* extinction—we must, simplistic as this may sound, *Wake Up* and *Act Now!* Here our *humanity* must become a burning center of love—love firstly for our endangered planet, and then for ourselves and our future generations. We must love this Mother Earth like the godlike beings we have become. (Imagine: what if we channeled our science and technology into healing the planet with the same can-do commitment that made the Apollo missions to the moon a success?) At the same time, we must love the Earth like the animals we will always be and like all the other creatures who are dependent on her and her health.

As Gellert indicated, the apocalypse the world is facing today is related to what he called my personal apocalypse insofar as both involve a transformation of the concept of God. I have already discussed how this is transforming on my part. For it to transform in the world would require a death-and-rebirth process more in the hearts of individuals than in the established ideology or dogma of their religions. It seems to me that a new concept of God would need to be realistic enough to somehow inspire both believers and nonbelievers. If I am any example, the conviction that such a concept is possible could only come from direct experience, and may not be altogether welcomed. Indeed, death and rebirth of whatever kind involve resistance and struggle.

With further regard to my personal apocalypse, it has penetrated to an intimate emotional level, asking me to change not only my concept of God but my experience of myself, of who I am. I have been challenged to not only think more deeply, but feel more deeply. One can think in solitude, but to feel demands connection with another.

Karen greeted me with a hug. I hadn't realized how much I needed it till I felt her arms squeezing me and the pressure of her hands on my back. I had been away for a short retreat to our country house in the mountains nearby and had just gotten back. After the preceding session with Gellert, I met with Karen and shared my dream with her, which until then she had only briefly heard about on the phone. I explained my need to take some time alone and sift through all that had happened in the past months—the separation, the surgery, the personal apocalypse and my meetings with Gellert. She understood. In a sense, I had created my own monastery in the heights, and now I was returning to my life below. Though still in a cloud of unknowing, I felt revitalized as I stood at the door of the house I once lived in. In my hands were gifts for my children and flowers for my estranged wife.

The children took delight in opening their gifts, and there followed the usual disengagement from the world as they became absorbed in their new toys and books. Karen and I talked a little, and then made dinner together. She prepared a salad while I barbecued chicken kebobs. Table talk with the kids consisted of the usual lively review of their daily and weekly events, some discussion of Rachel's piano lessons, and of course, the "promise" that has yet to be fulfilled: the puppy we will get as Ben's reward for his good behavior during his medical ordeal. After dinner, Rachel and I played cat's cradle and a game of checkers. Then both kids were bathed while listening to the Beatles (whom they love), and Ben got to wrestle me on the bed in the master bedroom. The trick was to wrestle just enough to tire him out, but then stop short of getting him too excited. Karen always let me know when Ben was about to cross that threshold. Finally came story time.

After the kids had fallen asleep I lit a fire. Karen and I sat on the couch across from it, each with a glass of wine. Inevitably, the conversation turned toward the paranormal incidents. "I understand their importance for you as a scientist," Karen said. "And maybe they're important for you psychologically too. Maybe you needed a miracle to break you out of your mold. It reminds me of Saint Augustine."

"How so?" I asked.

"He said that miracles are not contrary to nature, but only contrary to what we know about nature. His conversion to Christianity from Manichaeism involved a literary synchronicity somewhat like yours. He was experiencing a moment of intense grief, a crisis of doubt around his ability to give up his sexual addiction—he was quite a ladies' man. He was weeping with tears when he unexpectedly heard a child's voice singing from a neighboring house, *'tolle lege, tolle lege'*— 'pick it up, read it; pick it up, read it.' Though baffled, he intuited that this was a divine command to open a Bible that had been set down nearby and to read the first passage his eyes should fall upon. So, opening this Bible, his eyes fell upon a passage in which Jesus was exhorting his followers to give up indulgences of the flesh, particularly drunkenness and lustfulness. Augustine wrote that his heart was infused with certainty and that his gloom instantaneously vanished."

"If Augustine's addiction was the senses, mine was the mind, but in a limited way. Karen, I have always believed that the mind is a byproduct of the brain. Nothing in evolution indicates otherwise. Now it appears that this is true only on the level of physical evolution. It's as if the brain were a kind of transducer, plugging the mind into the physical plane, but there is another plane the mind plugs into beyond the known laws of physics, and if my

vision and dream are correct, it appears to be evolving
there, too."

"Buddhism has an interesting angle on evolution,
did you know that?"

"Gellert spoke about it a little—the bardos. But what
he described didn't sound like evolution to me. You
come back to your beginnings. You get reborn."

"Yes, but that's only part of it. The teaching that
comes from the Buddha is that our mind-continuum
takes many forms on the path to enlightenment. In his
view, the cosmos expands and contracts eternally, but
all sentient beings are on that path and will eventually reach enlightenment. Sounds a little like Teilhard,
doesn't it?"

"*Mind-continuum?* That's a curious concept. What
exactly does it mean?"

She didn't answer. "What are you smiling at?" I asked
with a mixture of humor and apprehension that she was
ridiculing me.

"You. I'm enjoying you. Do you know how long it
has been since I did that?"

I didn't want to hear the answer. Perhaps sensing this,
Karen didn't say more.

After some moments, she said, "Do you remember
that glacial lake we camped at in the Canadian Rockies,
the night we saw the northern lights?" Some twelve years
ago on a summer vacation we pitched a tent on a desolate
but beautiful shoreline facing the North Pole. We hadn't
seen the Aurora Borealis up till then and didn't expect to
this night either. A gentle, crystal-clear lake spread before
us like a sheet of ice. Suddenly the surface of the lake lit

up with dancing bars of light. Neither of us could figure out at first what it was, since the sky showed no activity. We intensely questioned what this phenomenon could be. Then we noticed just over the horizon across the lake a slight indication of the Aurora's electromagnetic field. Somehow it must have been casting a reflection on the lake even though a full view of it was obscured. Probably there was an optical explanation for this that we just weren't aware of.

"Yes, of course I remember," I said. "What made you think of that?"

"I like it when you ask questions. And when we ask them together."

"Well, I certainly have a lot of questions now."

"What part of your experience most grips you besides its paranormal aspect?"

"Those heavens Daniels showed me. They were stupendous, radiating not only a sense of purpose and joy but a humming energy that was soothing and . . . how can I describe it? . . . *Kind.*"

"As in 'lovingkindness'?"

"Yes."

"Maybe like the love all religions say is God?"

"Yes, maybe. It was as if the heavens were all burning centers of it. But I still find it hard to believe that worldly societies thrive on some other plane. Gellert suggested that this might be an allusion to something we just can't presently understand, or possibly the image of a new world order on this plane or an image of the collective unconscious itself.

"However," I added, "almost equally striking was that bizarre creature, the ortus. The way it looked at me. It was eerie. It wasn't a typical animal intelligence."

"What scared you about it, Richard?"

"I couldn't tell if it would attack us, if it was a wild animal, a predator. But even when I realized it had a special intelligence, its appearance frightened me."

"Was it ugly?"

"It was both. It was a beautiful monstrosity."

"That's an image you also find in the Renaissance, especially with Bosch. It shows how creation can be awesome beyond comprehension, and how the divine can manifest in monstrous ways."

A noise from the side jolted us. It was Ben, staring at us wide-eyed in his Spiderman pyjamas. I wasn't sure at first if he was sleep-walking. But then he made an ugly face, put his hand over his mouth as if to hold back laughter, abruptly turned around, and shot up the stairs to his room. Karen and I looked at each other and burst out laughing.

"I guess we wrestled too long," I said.

"Perhaps God is laughing at us with his ugly face," she said.

I stoked the fire, and poured us some more wine.

Karen then asked me whom did I think was my "better half" that Daniels said was waiting for me down in the meadow—was it her or the animal? I said that I naturally assumed it was her.

"I don't think so," she said. "I think it was the ortus. I'd never think of my soul mate as my other or better half, since I would want that person and me to be fully ourselves without needing another to complete us." She was a Renaissance romantic, but at the same time, utterly pragmatic.

Reaching for her hand, I took it to my lips and kissed it.

She said that she missed me while I was away, and that she wasn't just talking about the retreat to the country house. She said that my vision and dream felt like they came for her, too—not only because she had been in them but because they spoke to matters that were important to her. "The other day I googled Teilhard," she said. "Did you know that in 1955 he was living in residence at a Jesuit church in New York City? A few days before Easter he prayed to God to allow him to die on Easter Sunday if in his lifework he hadn't been wrong. He died of a heart attack that Easter Sunday."

"What do you think of that?" I asked her.

"I think it was an act of grace."

"Perhaps you are right," I said.

"You really think so?" she said, surprised.

"Yes. I know it could be argued that he willed this to happen that way, but on the other hand, was it necessarily any different than the synchronicities that happened to me?"

"So what does grace mean to you?"

"I'm looking at her right now."

She laughed.

"Do you know I fell in love with you in college," I said, "and am still in love with you?"

"Yes. But I wasn't sure if *you* knew. Or if you wanted to know." She leaned into me. "You could be a fool," she whispered.

Coda

A man should be able to say that he has done his best to form a conception of life after death, or to create some image of it—even if he must confess his failure. Not to have done so is a vital loss. . . . Psychic existence, and above all the inner images with which we are here concerned, supply the material for all mythic speculations about a life in the hereafter, and I imagine that life as a continuance in the world of images. Thus the psyche might be that existence in which the hereafter or the land of the dead is located.

— C. G. Jung

Love is a sacred reserve of energy; it is like the blood of spiritual evolution. . . . The day will come when, after mastering the winds, the waves, the tides and gravity, we shall harness for God the energies of love. And then, for the second time in the history of the world, man will have discovered fire.

— Pierre Teilhard de Chardin

How to Do Active Imagination

Jung's method of working with dreams involves not only a set of techniques but a distinct kind of meditation or contemplation. It is a segue to illumination.

(1) One technique of active imagination is to imagine the dream continuing from where it left off. You begin by reviewing the dream, "sinking into" it meditatively and as if it were actually reoccurring. Then you continue it to where you imagine it might have gone had it not ended where it did. Even if you suspect your conscious mind or ego is just "making it all up," if you're practicing this exercise meditatively, its content is still coming from *somewhere* and not unlikely from the unconscious. What started out as a single dream can develop into multiple episodes of active imagination that go well beyond the dream they began with.

(2) Another technique is to pick a character in the dream other than the dream ego (i.e., other than yourself in the dream) and write out a dialogue with them. The character may be a central one, but sometimes a seemingly peripheral character may hold the key to the dream's meaning. The character may also be nonhuman, e.g., an animal, a tree, or any other magical creature or object. In active imagination, as in the dreams it is based on, anything is possible.

In writing out the dialogue, the style used for plays—you get a turn to speak and then the character gets a turn—is usually adopted. You can ask or tell the character anything you like: why are they in the dream?; what do they want from you?; what do they know about you or your situation that you need to know?; etc. It can be very enlightening, even if disturbing, to hear them say things about you that you've never heard before or openly acknowledged. Thus, what makes such dialoguing an authentic, emotional interaction with the unconscious and not merely a cerebral activity of the ego is the ability to allow the character to really speak *their* mind as opposed to yours. To hear what they have to say, you must truly let go to the autonomous process of the imagination, to the living psyche. You may even imagine, when the character is speaking, that you are looking at yourself through their eyes. This is one way to get out of your ego's perspective and into theirs. Connecting to other perspectives that are latent in your psyche can make you more whole in your self-understanding and experience.

Here the question sometimes comes up, what does it mean when a famous historical person or celebrity enters our dreams or active imagination (for example, Teilhard de Chardin or in Jung's *Red Book* one of three possible figures from the third century named Ammonius)? All we can say for certain is that the unconscious part of the mind or psyche that reproduced their image seems to be reflecting something to us that this famous figure personifies. What is it about them that attracts us, or reversely, what is it about *us* that makes the unconscious want to draw our attention to them? That's the mystery we might wish to uncover. Mostly, they seem to carry the projection of our golden shadow when they are public figures we esteem and perhaps idealize; and they can carry the projection of our dark shadow when they appear as diabolical or threatening. What we say about them can be features of our own personal psychology as much as theirs, and what we often think we know about them is usually pure fantasy on our parts. I rarely recommend extensive active imagination with overly heroic or celebrity types, as their charisma tends to overshadow or altogether overwhelm the delicate process that makes active imagination work. Similarly, it is a general rule of thumb that practicing active imagination with living people we've actually known and who've played a role in our lives is not a good idea, as it can get into a kind of ancestor worship or voodoo thinking that serves our own desires rather than the unconscious's desires.

The same can be said for using active imagination as a way of communicating with the dead. This should be approached very carefully and for good reasons only, and rarely if ever at all, for what is important for us is to live our lives fully in the actual world we live in. As Thoreau said, "One world at a time." Active imagination is not to be turned into a form of channeling or a kind of séance. It is advisable not to go out of our way to initiate contact with the dead, but rather to deal with them only if and when they make contact with us. (Teilhard's appearance in our story is more as a cultural icon or figure of the religious imagination than as an emissary from the dead, even though the encounter with him takes place in the hereafter.)

A final technique of active imagination, one which Jung used a great deal in addition to the ones above, is to draw, paint, or sculpt the images in our dreams or *some* image that may not be in the dream itself yet captures its mood or essence. This visual technique may also bring the dream's core meaning into consciousness, though in a nonverbal way.

All of these techniques may be combined with each other. There are no hard and fast rules, and you must find your own preference and style. Indeed, Jung did not write a great deal about active imagination probably for this reason.

Lastly, it needs to be said that active imagination is a powerful tool and a most unpredictable form of meditation. If one does not have a strong, healthy ego that is well-grounded in the world, it may have dangerous and harmful effects. When in doubt, one should not practice it without the guidance of a therapist, and certainly, if what started out as an intriguing exploration makes us become dissociated or otherwise turns dark or diabolical, we should stop practicing it and consult a therapist. The psyche is a many-splendored thing, but not always a splendid one.

For further reading material, Jung's posthumously published *Red Book* (W. W. Norton & Co., 2009)—his verbal *and* visual account of his inner odyssey around the time of his break from Freud—provides a wonderful illustration of this method's ability to plumb the psyche's depths. He offers a more scholarly treatment of it in his 1916 essay, "The Transcendent Function" (in *The Structure and Dynamics of the Psyche*, Volume 8 of *The Collected Works of C. G. Jung*, Princeton University Press, 1978), as well as in a later work on alchemy ("The Conjunction," in *Mysterium Coniunctionis: An Inquiry into the Separation and Synthesis of Psychic Opposites in Alchemy*, Volume 14 of *The Collected Works of C. G. Jung*, Princeton

University Press, 1970). A more complete collection of Jung's essays on active imagination is Joan Chodorow's *Jung on Active Imagination* (Princeton University Press, 1997). Two excellent books further explaining how to do active imagination are Barbara Hannah's *Encounters with the Soul: Active Imagination as Developed by C. G. Jung* (Chiron Publications, Asheville, North Carolina, 2015; originally published by Sigo Press, Santa Monica, California, 1981) and Robert A. Johnson's *Inner Work: Using Dreams and Active Imagination for Personal Growth* (Harper & Row, New York, 1986). The latter of these is especially accessible. A special treatment of the similarity between active imagination and the meditation practiced by the alchemists is provided in Marie-Louise von Franz's *Alchemical Active Imagination* (Shambhala Publications, Boulder, Colorado, revised edition, 1997). On active imagination as a bridge to the dead, and how to walk this bridge without losing our grounding in the everyday world, I recommend Stephani L. Stephens's *C. G. Jung and the Dead: Visions, Active Imagination and the Unconscious Terrain* (Routledge, New York, 2019). Finally, for a soulful, poignant exploration of how active imagination can help us face our own death and connect with inner resources we didn't know we had, see *Appointment with the Wise Old Dog: Dream Images in a Time of Crisis* (a documentary produced by David Blum, with an Introduction by Yo Yo Ma, available on Amazon or at *www. davidblummusiciananddreamer.com*, 1998, 2010).

Appendix II
A Bibliographic Note

There may arise some confusion around the title of Teilhard de Chardin's key work, *The Phenomenon of Man*. The first English translation of this by Bernard Wall was published with this title by William Collins Sons & Co. (London) and Harper & Row (New York) in 1959, and revised in 1965. However, the original French edition, published by Éditions du Seuil (Paris) in 1955, was called *Le Phénomène Humain*, or *The Human Phenomenon*. (This is most likely what Jung read in 1961 when, in failing health shortly before his death, he described it as "a great book." His friend, Miguel Serrano, to whom he told this reports that "On the small table beside the chair where Jung was sitting, was a book called *The Human Phenomenon* by Teilhard de Chardin" [*C. G. Jung and Hermann Hesse: A Record of Two Friendships*, Schocken Books, New York, 1968, pp. 100–101].)

An improved English translation by Sarah Appleton-Weber, published in 1999 by Sussex Academic Press (Eastbourne, Great Britain and Chicago), reverts to the original title, *The Human Phenomenon*. I do not use that title in this book because my first reading of this seminal work was the translation by Wall. Also, many in the English-speaking world still refer to it as *The Phenomenon of Man*. However, all this said, I'm afraid that neither translation is the best introduction to Teilhard's thought should an introduction be desired, even though that book is his most penetrating and comprehensive. *The*

Future of Man (HarperCollins, New York, 1964) or *Christianity and Evolution* (Harcourt, San Diego, 1971) offers a more accessible introduction to his ideas. Probably the best introduction would be his more mystical and inspiring books, most notably *The Divine Milieu* (Harper & Row, New York, 1960) and *Hymn of the Universe* (Harper & Row, New York, 1961). *On Love & Happiness* (trans. J. M. Cohen, Harper & Row, San Francisco, 1984) is also uplifting. Many of Teilhard's books may be read online at Internet Archive (archive.org).

Acknowledgments

I am very grateful to Yvonne Paglia, my publisher, for her friendship over the years and for accepting this book into Nicolas Hays's fine collection of titles. As this is my third book to be published by Nicolas Hays, it feels like a homecoming for me.

James Wasserman, my gifted editor, did an exceptionally fine job with the cover, internal design, and other production details. As an accomplished author in his own right, we shared a special camaraderie. Sadly, Jim passed away shortly after completing the midwifing process of this book—his "final farewell," as Yvonne put it. Kathryn Sky-Peck, who was editor for one of my former Nicolas-Hays books, kindly helped with some final production matters.

Heartfelt thanks are due to my wise and talented agent, Kimberley Cameron, who has stuck with me over the years through thick and thin and with a confidence, faith, and optimism well beyond the call of duty.

JoAnn Culbert-Koehn, Barney Prentice, Steve Frank, Charles Zeltzer, Daniel Rothstein, John Dobbs, Aryeh Maidenbaum, Bradley TePaske, Marton Csokas, Jerry Barclay, Christophe Le Mouël, Caroline Davis, Chelsie Koppenhaver, Gilda Frantz, Harriet Friedman, and Katharine Bainbridge each contributed in their own way. I am indebted to one and all.

I remain deeply thankful, years after my operation, to my very knowledgeable and capable brain surgeon, Dr. Neil Martin, who looms large among the few people who dramatically affected the quality of my life. It should be noted that the surgeon mentioned in these pages is generic and in no way resembles him.

Finally, all quoted or referenced material falls under the categories of fair use. Nevertheless, grateful acknowledgment is made to the following: Sir Denys Wilkinson, "Matter and Sub-matter," in *The Listener* (a magazine established by the BBC), July 21, 1960. Melinda M. Snodgrass, "Up the Long Ladder," *Star Trek: The Next Generation*, Paramount Domestic Television, CBS, Season 2, Episode 18, May 22, 1989. Mona Simpson, "A Sister's Eulogy for Steve Jobs," *The New York Times*, Opinion Pages, October 30, 2011. Sonu Shamdasani, Introduction, in C. G. Jung, *Red Book: Liber Novus*, W. W. Norton, Philemon Series, New York, 2009 (incl. reference to Augustine's *Soliloquies* and Jung's quote on Nietzsche, the latter a private possession of Stephen Martin). Augustine, *Soliloquies and Immortality of the Soul*, ed. and trans. Gerard Watson, Aris & Phillips, Warminster, UK, 1990. T. S. Eliot, in "Dante," *Selected Essays by T. S. Eliot*, Harcourt Brace & Co., New York, 1932. Alan P. R. Gregory, *Coleridge and the Conservative Imagination*, Mercer University Press, Macon, GA, 2003. William Blake, "A Vision of the Last Judgment," in Alexander Gilchrist, *Life of William Blake with Selections from His Poems and Other Writings*, Vol. 2, Cambridge University Press, Cambridge, UK, 2010. Dante Alighieri, *The Divine Comedy*, in *The Portable Dante*, ed. Paulo Milano, trans. Laurence Binyon, Penguin Books, Viking Portable Library, New York, 1978 (*Paradiso*, XXII, ln. 151). Albert Einstein, "Science, Philosophy and Religion: A Symposium," 1941. On Jung reading Teilhard de Chardin: see bibliographic information on Miguel Serrano in Appendix II. Johann Wolfgang von Goethe, "The Holy Longing," in *The Rag and Bone Shop of the Heart: A Poetry Anthology*, trans. Robert Bly, ed. Robert Bly, Michael Meade, and James Hillman, Harper-Perennial, New York, 1993. Pierre Teilhard de Chardin, *Letters to Two Friends: 1926–1952*, New American Library, New York, 1968. Samuel Taylor Coleridge, *Samuel Taylor Coleridge: Selected Poetry and Prose*, ed. E. Schneder, Rinehart, Boulder, CO, 1951. *The Rubaiyat of Omar Khayyam*, trans. Edward FitzGerald, 1st and 5th editions, Dover, Mineola, NY, 1990. Doris Lessing, *Re: Colonized Planet 5, Shikasta*, Alfred A. Knopf, New York, 1979. D. H. Lawrence, *The White Peacock*, ed. Andrew Robertson, Cambridge University Press, Cambridge, UK, 1983. Gotthold Ephraim Lessing, *Emilia Galotti: A Tragedy in Five Acts*, Barron's Educational Series, Hauppauge, NY, 1959. C. G. Jung, *Memories, Dreams, Reflections*, Vintage Books/Random House, ed. Aniela Jaffé, trans. Richard and Clara Winston, New York, 1963. Pierre Teilhard de Chardin, *On Love & Happiness*, trans. J. M. Cohen, Harper & Row, San Francisco, 1984. Henry David Thoreau, in William J. Phillips, *One World at a Time: Reflections on Character and the Moral Wisdom of Henry David Thoreau*, Xlibris, Bloomington, IN, 2009.

Praise for Earlier Books by Michael Gellert

The Divine Mind: Exploring the
Psychological History of God's Inner Journey

WINNER OF THE NAUTILUS BOOK AWARD

"Michael Gellert reads God's inner journey from the pages of scripture—Jewish, Christian, and Muslim—into its continuation in three mystical traditions and on down to our own day. An engrossing account, enriched by Jungian psychology, that makes God's journey a persuasive metaphor for our own."

— JACK MILES, Pulitzer Prize-winning author of
God: A Biography

"In this fascinating account, Gellert applies depth psychology and trauma theory to Yahweh's inner journey from trauma to redemption, a journey that parallels the evolution of our consciousness as well. This creative, engaging book seems especially relevant to our time, when the Abrahamic religions and their patriarchal assumptions are so frequently in our daily news cycle—seeking transformation and redemption like the Yahwistic God himself."

— DONALD KALSCHED, author of *The Inner World of
Trauma* and *Trauma and the Soul*

"Michael Gellert offers a road map that leads from the mind's myriad projections to the enigmatic soul and its own origin. Crossing some fascinating and at times painful terrain, he brings the reader into silent realms of contemplation, and concludes his book on a joyful, mystical note. It is an intriguing book, to put it mildly."
— VRAJE ABRAMIAN, translator of *Nobody, Son of Nobody: Poems of Sheikh Abu-Saeed Abil Kheir* and *Winds of Grace: Poetry, Stories and Teachings of Sufi Mystics and Saints*

The Way of the Small: Why Less Is Truly More

WINNER OF SPIRITUALITY & PRACTICE'S BOOK AWARD
FOR ONE OF THE BEST SPIRITUAL BOOKS OF 2007

"This is a jewel of a book. There is a pearl inside it. Read the words closely, and you will discover that pearl—elusive, precious, and tiny."

— From the Foreword by THOMAS MOORE, author of
Care of the Soul and *Dark Nights of the Soul*

"Balancing our inner and outer worlds, this beautiful book is both deeply spiritual and eminently practical. It masterfully empowers us to thrive in a simple way in our overwhelmingly complex times. Original, eloquent, wise, and inspiring, this is an important book that should be read by everyone."

— ROBERT A. JOHNSON, author of *Inner Work* and
Owning Your Own Shadow

"A bold, persuasive book come to teach us how we can all be winners, with no losers, at the game of life."

— RABBI HAROLD KUSHNER, author of
When Bad Things Happen to Good People

Michael Gellert

America's Identity Crisis:
The Death and Rebirth of the American Vision
(Originally published as *The Fate of America*)

WINNER OF THE NAUTILUS BOOK AWARD

"Our nation leads the world in the race for ever-increasing technological capacity and excellence. Why is it we are not equally dominant in the race for spiritual excellence? This fascinating, insightful, psychological profile of the American psyche offers answers that both enlighten and stimulate."

— GOVERNOR MARIO CUOMO, author of
Why Lincoln Matters

"A large-scale analysis of this country on a par with Tocqueville . . . an important book. It raises serious questions about our country, makes perceptive observations about our culture, and provokes us to look inside ourselves in a critical, yet constructive, way."

— HOWARD ZINN, author of
A People's History of the United States

"This is a very fine book, written with erudition, conviction and a point of view that is always clear, without being dogmatic. It is not only an essential read for any American with a curiosity about our 'national character,' but also for citizens of the rest of the world who want an in-depth, accurate portrait of the American psyche."

— THOMAS SINGER, M.D., *Journal of Analytical Psychology*

Modern Mysticism:
Jung, Zen and the Still Good Hand of God

"A psychotherapist writes that rarest of works—a look at the wondrous and mysterious worlds of the unconscious mind, moving from the paranormal to the highest spiritual experience."
— SOPHY BURNHAM, author of *A Book of Angels*

"Gellert takes you with him, into the whale's belly and out! His experience in Calcutta is extraordinary—not to be wished for and not to be missed!"
— DIANE WOLKSTEIN, author of *The First Love Stories: From Isis and Osiris to Tristan and Iseult*

"An innovative and important approach to psychic phenomena. Challenges the present-day psychological conception of projections in a refreshing and thought-provoking manner."
— NATHAN SCHWARTZ-SALANT, author of *The Borderline Personality* and *Narcissism and Character Transformation*

About the Author

Photo © Norman Weinstein

MICHAEL GELLERT was born and raised in Montreal. The son of Hungarian Holocaust survivors, he was educated in rabbinic Judaism. Traveling at age nineteen overland from Europe to India and throughout the Indian subcontinent, he had a close brush with death, an experience described later in his first book, *Modern Mysticism*. He studied theology at Loyola College, Montreal (where he first learned of the ideas of Teilhard de Chardin and Jung), and trained with the renowned Zen master Kōun Yamada in Japan for two years. He earned master's degrees in religious studies and clinical social work, studied the psychological effects of mass media with Marshall McLuhan at the University of Toronto, and trained in couple therapy at the Ackerman Institute for the Family, New York. He served as a humanities professor at Vanier College, Montreal, and as a lecturer in religious studies at Hunter College of the City University of New York. He managed an employee assistance program for the City of New York and has been a mental health consultant for the University of Southern California and *Time* magazine.

A Jungian analyst practicing in Los Angeles and Pasadena, Gellert is a former Director of Training and currently an instructor at the C. G. Jung Institute of Los Angeles. He also leads a Jungian Writing Workshop. His other books include *The Way of the Small* (winner of Spirituality & Practice's Book Award for One of the Best Spiritual Books of 2007), *America's Identity Crisis*, and *The Divine Mind* (the latter two each receiving a Nautilus Book Award). He lectures widely on psychology, religion, and contemporary culture. His website is *michaelgellert.com*.

A Note to Our Readers

IBIS PRESS / NICOLAS HAYS is dedicated to to providing the finest spiritual literature available today. We specialize in publishing books from both classic and modern sources that outline the basis and development of the world's Mystery Traditions. Our subjects include Depth Psychology, Alchemy, Astrology, Magick, New Age thought, Women's Mysteries, and the many other paths of human striving for union with the Infinite. For more information, contact us us at *info@ibispress.net* or *info@nicolashays.com*

Distributed by Redwheel/Weiser, LLC.
65 Parker St. • Ste. 7 • Newburyport, MA 01950
www.redwheelweiser.com